From Earth to Health

How to Grow, Harvest and Store Your Own Organic Food for Optimal Nutrition

DAVID SCHLEICHER

Printed in the United States of America

Library of Congress Control Number: 2012919949

Createspace Independent Publishing Platform

North Charleston, SC

Terms of Use

You are given a nontransferable, *personal* use license to this book. You cannot distribute it or share it with other individuals.

Also, there are no resale rights or private label rights granted when purchasing this book. In other words, it's for your own personal use only.

From Earth to Health

How to grow, harvest and store your
own organic food for optimal nutrition

I'd like to dedicate this book to my granddaughter Heidi, who even at the age of 6 has shown a love for growing things. I would also like to give special thanks to my wife Jan, and to Teresa Lambert for her helpful editing.

Table of Contents

Introduction

From earth to health. It sounds too simple to be true, kind of like the old saying, "You are what you eat." The truth is that there is ample scientific evidence to prove that one of the biggest elements to a healthy life is the eating of fresh, organically grown produce—especially if it is from your own garden. I believe that the only real reason we eat is to provide us with good health.

Farming in North America has become a large-scale corporate affair. Fifty percent of all the food production in the United States comes from only 2 percent of the farms. Maybe an even more telling statistic is that we now have more prisoners in this country than farmers. Hundreds, if not thousands, of acres are planted with a single crop, which is grown in the same fields year after year. Since this is not natural, corporate agribusiness resorts to chemical fertilizers and copious amounts of herbicides, pesticides, and fungicides in order to produce a salable crop. According to Joel Salatin in *Everything I Want to Do Is Illegal*, industrial food production is now threatening our health. Obesity, diabetes, heart disease, cancer, and food-borne pathogens like E. coli and salmonella were almost unheard of before 1900, when industrialized food production started.

We have known the solution for at least twenty-four hundred years now. That was when Hippocrates wrote, "Let thy food be thy medicine, and thy medicine be thy food." For all of our high-tech science today, we have lost sight of the simple truths of good health.

According to Raymond Francis in *Never Be Sick Again*, the biggest health problem in America today is malnutrition. So how can this be, when obesity is epidemic as well? The truth is that most Americans are *overfed but undernourished.*

Raymond says that there is only one disease: malfunctioning cells. And there are only two causes of malfunctioning cells: a lack of nutrition and toxicity. Although this may sound simplistic, I agree with it wholeheartedly. I believe the best way to ensure that each cell in your body has the right nutrients, as well as the least amount of toxicity, is to eat fresh, locally grown organic produce. A further benefit is that many of our leafy green vegetables are able to bind up some of these toxins and flush them from the body. Parsley and cilantro in particular are very good at cleansing heavy metals from the body.

Oh, my goodness, I've used the O word several times already. I say this only a little tongue-in-cheek because the USDA regulates very tightly who may use the O word to describe a product (at least if you have any intention of selling the produce). Now I don't want to get off on a rant here, but when people ask me if my farm is *certified organic*, my usual reply is, "No, I would never stoop that low." The reason for that response is that the USDA has an entire list of what the agency refers to as "synthetic substances allowed for use on organic crop production" (section 205.621). These include such chemicals as peracetic acid, sucrose octanoate esters, streptomycin, and tetracycline. If I were making the rules for organic crop production, my list of approved synthetic substances would be blank. Also, it only takes three years to convert from nonorganic production on a farm to organic—and those toxic chemicals can remain in the soil and ecosystem much longer than that.

I don't want you to get the wrong idea here that I am against USDA-certified organic foods. As a matter of fact, I try very hard to make sure that any produce I do purchase is certified organic because I believe it is much less toxic than anything not certified organic. But I would *never* use any synthetic chemicals on any crops that I grow.

In addition to growing crops organically, I follow two other gardening philosophies. The first is permaculture. David Holmgren, co-creator of the concept, defines permaculture as *"consciously designed landscapes which mimic the patterns and relationships found in nature, while yielding an abundance of food, fiber, and energy for provision of local needs."* Some of the core design principles of permaculture are: to catch and store energy, to use renewable resources, to produce no waste, to integrate rather than segregate, and to use and value diversity.

I think the key here is to mimic nature. For example, lettuce does not naturally grow in water and tomatoes don't grow upside down. There is diversity in a forest or meadow but not in a monoculture.

The second philosophy is the biointensive method. Simply put, the *biointensive method focuses on maximum yields from a minimum area of land, while simultaneously improving the soil.* Some of the tenets of this philosophy are double digging, companion planting, calorie farming, and using open pollinated seeds. If you would like to know more about this, see John Jeavons's book *How to Grow More Vegetables*.

The advantages of eating locally grown organic produce are:

1. *Quality.* It is just plain tough to beat the taste and texture of a garden-fresh carrot or tomato. Most of the commercial farming is done on land that has been continuously farmed for many years and even decades. The high cost of fertilizer results in the minimum amount being used to get a decent harvest. The result has been a

constant decline in the nutrient value of most of our common produce—as much as 50 percent in some studies. The 1992 Rio Earth Summit found that agricultural soils in the United States have been depleted of 85 percent of their minerals in the last hundred years. And the intensive chemical and monoculture commercial farming of the last twenty years has probably made it even worse.

2. *Freshness.* Most fruits and vegetables start to degrade the moment they are picked. Commercial produce varieties are chosen for their yield and shipping ability rather than what tastes the best and has the highest nutrient value. They are usually picked long before optimum ripeness and therefore are missing some of the best nutrients and flavor.

3. *Safety.* With the recent outbreaks of salmonella and E.coli in everything from peanut butter to lettuce to tomatoes, it behooves all of us to be very careful about what we eat. Even buying commercially grown organic produce does not ensure safety because it might have been shipped with other fruit or vegetables that have been contaminated.

Raw vegetables are much more nutritious for you than cooked vegetables. A temperature of approximately 118 degrees starts to break down the enzymes present in the raw form. Cooking also removes many of the beneficial nutrients. Obviously vegetables like winter squash and potatoes are not very good raw, and there are some vegetables that increase their nutrient value when cooked. For example, Italian researchers have discovered that steamed broccoli contained certain anti-cancer compounds not found in the raw form and boiled carrots contained higher levels of carotenoids. Our personal goal is to eat two-thirds of our fruits and vegetables raw.

The information and data I provide here is based on four decades of growing fruits and vegetables in a northern climate. It is *not* based on something I read in a book or tried once. It is based on what has worked for me over a long period. My current garden is in zone 4 of the USDA Plant Hardiness Zone Map, where minus-twenty-degree temperatures are typical during a normal winter. I have experienced frosts in every month of the year, and our native soil is terrible. The purpose in telling you this is to show that good garden harvests are possible even in less-than-desirable conditions.

If you have a small yard, then do the best you can with a tiny garden. If you live in an apartment or condo, try some container gardening. And if by chance you live in a cave, try to cultivate a friendship with someone who will let you garden on his or her property in return for some fresh vegetables. If growing things is just not in your genes, you can still use this book to find some fresh, local produce to preserve, store, and eat.

This book has something for everyone, no matter what your skill level. Whether you are a brand new gardener or have years of experience, I hope you are able to learn something valuable.

My goal is to help you grow, harvest, store, and prepare your own fruits and vegetables as simply and economically as possible. Please know that the information I present is not necessarily *the way* to do this, but *a way* I have found that works for me.

Chapter 1

THE BASICS

Vegetable gardening in its most basic form is actually pretty easy. Just scratch up some soil, plant a few seeds, add some water, pick a few weeds, and then thin the crop and wait for the harvest. Although this method will work for a few hardy vegetables, it will not work well for the majority of plants. It seems that the more these plants are bred, the less hardy they become. With the investment of a little knowledge, time and effort, you can significantly increase the quality and quantity of your garden.

A garden needs five things to grow successfully: soil, water, sunshine, appropriate temperature, and either a seed or a transplant.

SOIL

Although all of the items listed above play their own important role, the soil probably has the biggest impact on the final plant quality. Good health depends on wholesome food, and this can only come from fertile soil. *Fertile soil is the secret to good plant quality, and compost is the key to fertile soil.* Compost is nothing more than the breakdown of any organic material. For most home gardeners, this would include things like grass clippings, leaves, weeds, and kitchen waste. Generally the more organic material worked into your soil, the better. The easiest way to do this is to duplicate nature's system by putting the organic material on top of the soil and letting the worms and other soil organisms mix it in.

Now I know that hydroponics (growing plants in a nutrient solution without soil) is becoming more popular and certainly produces big crops, but I believe that growing plants in good old-fashioned dirt is the only way to go. Nature has designed plants to be rooted in soil, and many vegetables will die if their roots are too wet.

For many gardens compost will provide most of the nutrients that the plants require. Adding just a few amendments can really boost yields and provide mineral-dense fruits and vegetables. I use a homemade, completely organic fertilizer blend that is simple to make. I take a fifty-pound bag of Fertrell 3-2-3 organic fertilizer and add ten pounds of kelp meal and twenty-five pounds of Azomite. This eighty-five pounds of minerals is enough for one thousand square feet of garden. Kelp meal is seaweed harvested from the ocean and does a wonderful job of increasing the biological activity as well as helping to break down the organic material. It is also a good source of iodine, which is lacking in most soils. Azomite is a natural rock material mined in Utah that provides sixty-seven minerals and trace elements. It is important to understand that this mix is slow-releasing and should be added to your soil in the fall or early spring. I vary the application rate depending on what vegetables will go in a bed, but the average is about three pounds per four-foot by eight-foot bed. If I am planting carrots I'll add a little greensand to the mix, and if I'm growing beets I'll add a little boron.

If you have access to ashes from a wood stove or fireplace, they are great for your garden in four different ways. They are a good organic fertilizer, adding phosphorus, potassium, and many trace minerals. The ashes are also a good soil conditioner, helping to break up the clods in clay soils. Wood ashes are an organic pesticide when scattered on top of the ground, helping to deter slugs, snails, and cutworms. And lastly, biochar (the charcoal-looking nuggets) greatly increases the efficiency of fertilizers and enhances plant yield. Wood ashes do raise the pH of the soil, so you should not use them around acid-loving plants like blueberries.

Another issue with soil is that of aeration. Plant roots require air to grow, and a highly compacted soil will stunt plant growth. The best answer is to grow a garden in raised beds (so that the soil is never walked on) and to turn in compost, which adds texture and fluffs up the soil.

I do not use, nor do I recommend, any synthetic or chemical fertilizers! Only providing a quick fix to begin with, synthetic fertilizers can burn the plant roots, destroy beneficial organisms, and build up salts. They are also made almost exclusively from petrochemicals.

I have come to the conclusion that plants share a trait with us humans. We both have a natural ability to withstand infection and disease if we have the proper nutrition and do not poison ourselves with toxins.

WATER

It may seem that watering plants would be a simple task. In reality it is a bit more complicated, and it's important to know how plants utilize water. Most of the water used by a plant comes through its root system. A single full-grown tomato plant can have a root system about four feet in diameter and four feet deep. It is also key to understand that most of the nutrients the plant needs come dissolved in the water it takes in.

The secret is to get just the right amount of water to that whole root system. The way to do this is through deep, periodic watering rather than more frequent shallow watering. The goal should be to get the top six to eight inches of soil rather wet. I find that for most plants about one to two inches of water per week is sufficient. Leaves that are wilting or turning brown may have insufficient water. Leaves turning yellow indicate overwatering.

Rain water at ambient temperature is the perfect water to use. (I use rain barrels to collect water.) Cold, chemically treated city water is the worst. The chlorine and fluoride leech into the soil, and the cold water chills the plants and roots. Unfortunately that is the only water available to most gardeners, so we are stuck with it.

Most gardening literature would have you water early in the morning, supposedly to prevent mold and fungus. I prefer to water in the early evening for several reasons. Most of the plant growth occurs at night so I want to get the proper amount of water to the root system then. The warm ground also helps to temper the water and warm it before it reaches the roots.

SUNSHINE

Most vegetables require an average of at least six hours of sun per day to grow properly. Fruiting plants like tomatoes and peppers need about eight hours of sun per day, and will only do better with increased amounts. These six hours should occur during the peak hours between 10:00 a.m. and 4:00 p.m. A full view of the southern sky will ensure that the garden is getting enough light.

Check the areas that you want to garden to make sure there is no shade sneaking in from neighboring structures or trees.

TEMPERATURE

The temperature of the soil is a crucial determining factor in plant growth. Warm air temperatures but cool soil temperatures will cause the plants to grow very slowly or even become stunted. Virtually all seeds require a soil temperature of at least fifty degrees to germinate, and many need at least sixty-five degrees. Most of the vegetables that are transplanted (like tomatoes and peppers) need a soil temperature of at least sixty degrees.

In my cool climate, it helps to warm the soil ahead of planting by using clear or black plastic. I set all of my transplants through a black mat that allows air and moisture to pass through but does not allow weeds to grow.

Within the normal range of growing conditions, every ten-degree increase in the soil temperature will double plant growth.

SEEDS

Planting the right seeds at the right time is probably the most over-looked part of successful gardening. The seed is the spark of life, and just like in humans and animals, good genes can go a long way.

Most people end up buying seed-rack seeds in the hardware store or supermarket, which contain poorly selected, nonproductive variet-ies or those with poor germination rates.

Because of my short growing season, I generally have only a brief window of time when each crop may be started. For a few vegetables, I may get repeated chances; but even then the window lasts only for a couple of weeks.

I buy most of my seeds from Johnny's Select Seeds. The company does germination trials twice a year and puts the results on every pack. I have had great results with Johnny's seeds.

WHAT TO GROW?

This question stymies most new gardeners. The list of seeds and plants to grow can be overwhelming. My advice is to keep it simple, work on balanced nutrition, focus on what grows best in your particular soil and climate, and have fun.

Here is my list of vegetables ranked by how easy they are to grow. This ranking takes into account the level of soil fertility required as well as thinning, weeding, and watering requirements.

Easy

- beans
- beets
- carrots
- herbs
- kale
- lettuce
- peas
- radishes
- spinach
- Swiss chard

Medium

- basil
- Brussels sprouts
- cabbage
- corn
- cucumbers
- eggplant
- garlic
- kohlrabi
- potatoes
- rutabagas
- squash
- tomatoes

Difficult

- asparagus
- cantaloupe
- cauliflower
- celery
- leeks
- onions
- peppers

Obviously you should plant vegetables that you like to eat. If you are a new gardener, stick with the first two categories until you start feeling comfortable with your skills.

OTHER CONSIDERATIONS

I have deliberately not talked about plant diseases. The reason is that following my gardening methods will lead to healthy soil and plants, and you will deal with few diseases. If you do get some sort of fungus or wilt, the best thing to do is talk to some experienced gardeners in your area to see how they deal with the problem. It is this same reason that I really don't worry about soil pH, which is the measure of the acid/ alkaline balance. Taking the appropriate steps necessary for proper soil fertility will allow the pH to fall in line.

Crop rotation is one very important feature of a successful and lasting garden. Vegetables are very specific in the particular nutrients they take from the soil, and planting in the same bed year after year depletes these nutrients and causes a deficiency. Also, some of the diseases and pests that typically don't bother a healthy plant can build up in the soil and overwhelm the plants.

The key is to plant a different crop each year in each bed. The nightshade family (tomatoes, eggplant, peppers, and potatoes) are the biggest offenders. None of these should ever follow one another in a good crop rotation. I try to plant light-feeding plants following the year of heavy feeders. Keep track of what you plant each year, and what part of the garden it's planted in.

Chapter 2

COMPOSTING

**Here is an example of a three bin compost pile
with the finished bin on the left.**

Fertile soil is the secret to good plant quality, and compost is the key to fertile soil. Yes, I know I've said that already, but is it starting to sink in yet? Compost is nothing more than the breakdown of any organic material. It is the process by which biodegradable materials, such as grass clippings, leaves, manure, and household wastes, are turned into a crumbly soil-like substance by combining them with air, water, and nitrogen. Modern methods of composting are nothing more than the speeding up of the natural decomposition process. Composting is all about giving back to the land what it has given to you and recycling those organic materials back into your garden to start the cycle all over again.

According to Steve Solomon in *Organic Gardener's Composting*, "Fertility...is the ability to produce at the highest recognized level of yield, crops of quality which, when consumed over long periods by animals or man, enable them to sustain health, bodily condition and high levels of production without evidence of disease or deficiency of any kind."

Unfortunately composting has gotten something of a bad name in the past. Many people believe compost smells bad, attracts rats and other vermin, and is a breeding ground for all sorts of bugs, snakes, and pests. The truth is that a properly built compost pile will cause none of these problems. I have been composting for more than thirty years with great success, and I just cringe when I see people sending good organic refuse to the landfill. Isn't it ironic that these same people who are throwing their organic matter away are the ones who bring bags of fertilizer home from the store? It's also important to know that even if you don't do everything just right, you'll still end up with some pretty usable compost.

Compost provides three important functions:

1. *The addition of organic matter, or humus, increases the fertility of the soil.* This is accomplished by the release of nutrients upon

the decomposition of the organic materials. This food source is not only for plants but for the bacteria, fungi, and other beneficial organisms like earthworms. Most of the plant nutrients and trace minerals have a positive electrical charge. Humus is negatively charged, therefore attracting these nutrients. Also, the humic acid given off from the humus dissolves the minerals and allows them to be taken up by the plant roots. This organic mixture then releases the nutrients slowly over a period of several months to several years. *In reality we feed the soil, and then the soil feeds our plants.*

2. *It improves the structure of the soil.* If the soil is too compacted it becomes very difficult for the roots to spread out. If it is too open, then the soil does not retain moisture nearly as well. A healthy soil is key to healthy plants. Insects, parasites, and fungi like to feed on sick plants.

3. *Compost acts as a mulch and ground cover to preserve water and maintain a more even ground temperature.*

WHAT CAN YOU COMPOST?

Here are a few of the most common items that you can compost:

- leaves
- grass clippings and weeds
- pine needles
- hay or straw
- shredded newspaper
- sawdust
- manures
- seaweed (kelp)

- feathers

- human urine (It's sterile!)

- kitchen scraps

- coffee grounds and tea bags

- wood ashes

- eggshells

It is important not to add any of these items if they have been treated with herbicides or pesticides, especially grass clippings.

Here are some materials to avoid putting in a compost pile:

- coal or charcoal ashes

- colored or glossy paper

- diseased plants

- pet or human feces

- meat scraps or grease

HOW DO I GET STARTED?

First you want to figure out which method to use. Here are the four most common methods:

Pile

This is the easiest method. Just put all of your organic components into a pile, and let nature and time do their thing. This will result in usable compost, but it will take longer (one to two years) and will not have high nutrient value.

Bin

In this method you would build some sort of structure to contain the ingredients. This is the method I use most often because it is much easier to *layer* all of the different items.

Sheet

This is where you layer the ingredients over a wide area. It works great for a new garden area if you have the time to let the items break down. The downside is that it does not generate the necessary heat to kill the weed seeds and pathogens.

Tumbler

This is the commercial unit (usually made of plastic) that you rotate to tumble the material. I find this type expensive and only able to make small quantities of compost.

Second you want to find a good place for the compost pile. It should be close to a source of water as well as within a reasonable distance from your garden. Also, it helps if the location is accessible by vehicle in case you are able to get manures or other items delivered. I recommend a fixed area of your yard for the composting operation.

And lastly, where are you going to get all of the organic materials? Every household will generate organic materials that can go into the compost bin, but will it be enough? For a compost pile to develop enough heat to kill weed seeds and other pathogens, it should be in an area at least three feet wide by three feet long and three feet high. That's a lot of organic material! Do you have neighbors who throw away their leaves and grass clippings? Do you know any farmers or ranchers who would let you have some manure? How about a landscaping or tree service that needs to get rid of some organic materials?

When I am gathering my materials, I have three criteria:

1. Are they free of all chemicals?

2. Are they diverse? I try to get as many different types of plants, manures, and leaves as I can. For manures I use horse, goat, and cow manure—and only from people I know and trust to get the manure from pastured animals. I will intentionally cut grass from various areas on the property to get a good variety.

3. Are they local? My goal is to get all of the materials from my property, and so far my property can generate everything but the manures.

BUILDING THE COMPOST PILE

Once you have all your materials and a place to put your compost, it's time to build your first pile. There are five keys to this process:

1. *Diversity.* The more varied the ingredients, the richer the compost will be in nutrients.

2. *Carbon-to-nitrogen ratio*. Try to get a ratio of about twenty-five or thirty to one. There are many scientific ways to calculate this, but I'll give you the easy way shortly.

3. *Mixing*. Mix and blend the ingredients together.

4. *Moisture*. Be sure you have the proper amount.

5. *Inoculant*. Usually this will be some sort of soil or finished compost.

I usually start a new pile with my coarsest materials, like big weeds or cornstalks. This tends to provide more aeration to the pile. Then I will alternate approximately two- to three-inch layers of green materials and four to six inches of brown materials. I like to use a lot of horse or cow manure in my piles because they are rich in nitrogen. I also use carbon materials (usually straw or sawdust) and beneficial bacteria. After putting down a couple layers of each, I'll add some inoculant and then water the pile thoroughly. As mentioned above, the activator can be as simple as some soil or old compost. After I've done several layers, I take my pitchfork and blend the materials together, adding a shovelful of wood ashes. Then I just keep layering and blending and watering until I've filled the bin or gotten the pile as big as I want it.

After a lot of experimenting over the years, I have determined that the optimum size for a compost pile is about four feet wide by four feet long and four feet high. If it gets much bigger than that, it is harder to handle. Additionally, creating too large of a pile can result in poor aeration because the excess weight causes the pile to compress too much, preventing oxygen from reaching the center and bottom of the pile.

A compost thermometer can track the progress of the decomposition process, but the old-fashioned way of sticking your hand into the center of the pile also works. Just be aware that a good compost pile can get very hot—mine will regularly hit 140 to 150 degrees. It generally takes a few days for the bacteria and enzymes to start doing their job and begin raising the pile's temperature.

If you do nothing after this point, you will have usable compost in about six to nine months. If you turn and mix the pile every few days after the temperature drops to about one hundred degrees, you can have good compost in as little as three months. In each of these cases, the organic material will not be completely decomposed and you will see occasional bits of stems and leaves, especially in the outer edges of the pile.

If your pile does not heat up to at least 120 degrees, it is almost always due to not having enough green material and/or the pile is too dry. There should be enough water in the pile that it approximates the feel of a wrung-out sponge. Fresh grass clippings are the best thing to add to get your pile to start generating heat because they are high in nitrogen (the green part) and also quite moist.

An odor from the pile or a temperature that is too high (it can actually get so hot that you will find a gray ash in the center) is usually an indication of too much green material and/or too much moisture. Adding some dry leaves and turning the pile will remedy this issue.

For the best quality compost in the shortest amount of time, organic items in the pile should be as small and mixed up as possible. I have experimented with putting everything through a chipper shredder, alternating between brown and green items. This shredding process turns everything into tiny pieces and does a great job of mixing things together. If you then turn the pile every three days, you can have pretty nice compost in about one month. I don't do this because it is very time-intensive.

LEAF MOLD

If this whole composting process is a little daunting for you, or if you want to add something else to your soil amendment toolbox, it might be worth making leaf mold. Although it sounds bad, it is easy to do and very beneficial.

Leaf mold is nothing more than partially decomposed leaves. There are several benefits to making and using leaf mold. First, it is very easy to make. Throw a bunch a leaves into a big pile or bin - I generally do a pile about 5 feet in diameter and 5 feet high. Let them sit for two to three years and you will have a rich, dark brown and sweet smelling soil amendment.

Second, it is a soil amendment extraordinaire. It can hold up to 500 per cent of its' own weight in water.

Third, it improves soil structure and provides a wonderful habitat for earthworms and beneficial bacteria.

Chapter 3

RAISED BEDS

Terraced garden with raised bed boxes.

I like to garden in raised beds more than any other method and here are my reasons:

- The soil in raised beds does not get compacted because you never need to walk on it.

- The soil warms faster in the spring, allowing you to plant earlier.

- You will not have to lean over and bend as much.

- You can tailor your soil to the particular type of plants for each bed.

- They require less maintenance in the long run.

- They make it easier to attach floating row covers or clear plastic for extending the growing season.

I will admit that the biggest negative for growing in raised beds is that they need more water. The warmer soil temperature and more intensive planting require more moisture.

So how do you construct a raised bed? Any method that contains soil above the normal ground level will work. You can use rocks, logs, lumber, hay bales, or bricks. You can also just mound up the soil, but erosion will be an issue with this method.

I use rough-sawn cedar lumber that is either two inches by six inches or two inches by eight inches by eight feet long, which I get from a local Amish sawmill. Three of these pieces of lumber will make one box that is approximately fifty inches by one hundred inches. Dimensional lumber from a lumberyard is only two and five-eighths inches by five and three-eighths inches by ninety-six inches long. The rough-sawn lumber will be a full two inches by six inches (or eight inches) and is usually at least one hundred inches long.

I cut one of the pieces exactly in half and screw the box together with deck screws. As of this writing, one of these four foot by eight foot boxes costs about twenty dollars and will last about twenty years or so.

Next, place the box in the desired position, preferably with the long side pointing due south. I believe in allowing ample room for the root system, so I dig out and amend the soil down to about twelve inches below ground level. You should level the box to ensure proper drainage and then add soil to the top of the box. I know that this requires a lot more work and compost, but trust me that it will be worth it for the next twenty years.

In all the beds that I will plant with heat-loving crops, such as tomatoes, peppers, eggplant, and squash, I cover the frame with black landscape fabric. I staple it to the frame just like I'm wrapping a present. This warms the soil even more, helps conserve soil moisture, and cuts the weeding down to nothing.

Raised beds require very little maintenance after the original construction. I pull off the fabric after the growing season and store it for the next year, digging in an inch or two of compost. I try not to disturb the soil until I plant the next spring. This helps to control weeds in the boxes that do not get the landscape fabric.

I have been experimenting with another technique called *hugelkultur*. This is a German word that, literally translated, means *mound culture*. I like to pronounce the *hugel* part like *Google*, although my German friends insist that is not quite right. I like the concept because it combines two of my favorite gardening techniques: raised beds and composting.

Hugelkultur is the practice of using rotting wood to create raised beds. The woody debris (sticks, branches, and logs) are stacked onto a pile and covered with organic material like weeds and leaves and finally a layer of soil. These mounds can be any size, but bigger is better.

The hugelkultur beds have all of the previously mentioned advantages of raised beds, *plus* all of these:

1. The decaying wood acts like a giant sponge, holding a tremendous amount of water.

2. Fungi begin feeding on this large amount of carbon and releases nutrients into the soil.

3. For the first few years, the composting action will warm the soil and lengthen your growing season.

4. The small air spaces among the pieces of wood greatly increase the aeration level of the soil.

5. As the wood shrinks over time, it will create more air pockets and therefore become self-tilling.

6. This method has been demonstrated to eliminate or drastically reduce the fertilization and watering requirements.

7. Old, rotting wood can be utilized as a resource instead of burned or disposed of.

8. If you are a believer in global warming, this is pure carbon sequestration!

Most kinds of wood can be used in a hugelkultur bed, with the exception of those that don't break down well or are toxic. I would not use cedar, locust, or black walnut wood. Also, the older the wood the better. If your pile was made with predominantly new wood, the high carbon content would probably leech some of the nitrogen from your soil and plants.

I have built four hugelkultur beds this year, and so far they have been quite successful. I planted squash on one of the mounds and did not have to water it after July, even though we had a very dry summer.

Chapter 4

WEEDING

Celery grown through black landscape fabric.

I admit it. I hate weeding. So much so, in fact, that I spend a lot of time trying to find ways to minimize the amount of weeds in the garden. I do think it helps to remember that a weed is just a plant that happens to be growing where you don't want it to. In fact, many weeds are beneficial to the soil; and the worst thing you can do is to have bare soil. What I like to do is *weed the soil and not the plants*. Here are a few of the ways that I go about this:

Composting

A properly built compost pile will heat to a temperature that will kill all weed seeds. On early-planted spring beds, I incorporate this compost into the soil the preceding fall. On the midsummer beds, I till in the compost in early spring.

Mulches

I use black landscape fabric on the beds anytime I can (usually with tomatoes, peppers, eggplant, squash, kale, sweet potatoes, and Brussels sprouts). On the beds where the fabric doesn't make sense, I use organic mulches like dried grass clippings and shredded leaves. Not only do these mulches prevent most weeds, but they also retain moisture and warm up the ground in the spring while cooling it off in midsummer.

Solarizing

This is a fantastic way to control weeds in the garden. This consists of wetting the bed (and yes, this is a good thing) and then placing a piece of clear plastic over the bed for a period of at least four to six weeks. This solarizing step typically follows the amendment of the soil with compost.

I still do some traditional weeding, but I keep telling myself that I am just raising some green matter for the compost pile...

Chapter 5

BUGS AND CRITTERS

Colorado potato beetles.

The most common reason people give for not wanting to garden organically is dealing with bugs and animals. This topic could fill an entire book by itself, so I'll just provide the basics here and show you how I deal with the problem.

We live in the middle of the woods, and all the birds and animals think that my garden is a buffet put out just for them. I think I have tried every known deterrent—including human hair, soap shavings, garlic, and the commercial sprays—and none of them have worked reliably. After years of experimenting, I ended up with an electric fence with the first strand about an inch off the ground and the fourth strand at a height of six feet. This keeps everything out of the garden except the birds, and I really don't have many problems with them.

The insects are a whole other problem. Every year is different, but the battle is always fought the same way. The key is to inspect your plants every day to catch the invaders early. If you can deal with the adults before they lay their eggs, your fight will be infinitely easier.

I have a four-pronged approach for dealing with insects:

1. Grow the best and strongest plants that you can. Just like in the human world, predators tend to prey on the weak.

2. Research the bugs that are common to your area, and have a plan in place to deal with them at the first sign of infestation.

3. Be extremely vigilant in inspecting the plants on a daily basis to catch the problem before it gets out of hand.

4. At the first sign of damage or appearance of an insect, I'll start with the least-invasive remedy. Typically this would be to physically remove any of the insects, larvae, or eggs. In most cases this is enough to contain the problem. If it doesn't I go to the next step, which is usually some sort of spray. Garlic/soap solutions and neem oil are two of my favorites.

Chapter 6

EXTENDING YOUR SEASON

My homemade sixteen-foot by twelve-foot greenhouse.

For those of us who live in areas with short summers and long winters, it is worthwhile to find ways to get more from our gardens. I like to break it into two distinct seasons: the growing season and what I call the *suspended animation* season.

In the extended growing season, we are trying to create a warmer environment to trick our plants into believing that they are really living in a warmer climate. This entails adding some sort of protection to prevent frosts and freezes. In the suspended animation season, we are keeping the plants alive to allow us to have fresh produce, but there really is not enough light to allow the vegetables to grow much.

Here are the three key steps to extending your season:

Site Selection

You should look for the sunniest spots in the garden, where you can start growing earlier and keep the plants going longer. I have found the best time to do this is in the early spring when you can see the areas where the snow melts first. Another aspect of site selection is the wind. Young plants have a difficult time with the wind, and the coverings can be damaged. Know your prevailing winds and find the most protected spots to start with.

Crop Selection

It is much easier to extend your season with crops that typically grow well in cool weather, like spinach and kale. If you are going to try this method with warm-weather vegetables like tomatoes or peppers, it will really pay off to find the varieties that are more cold-tolerant. Most seed catalogs will provide information on varieties that do well in cool temperatures. I have found through a lot of trial and error the varieties that perform best in my area.

Coverings

The first and simplest covering method is the good old-fashioned way of putting blankets on the plants at night when frost is expected. The blankets need to be dry, and it is more effective if you can prevent the blankets from coming into direct contact with the plants.

The second method is to use a commercial row cover (such as Agribon). It is also called garden fabric or floating row cover. These covers come in various weights, and the typical fabric will provide frost protection down to about twenty-eight degrees. They have other advantages, too. Row covers allow air and water to pass through and are very effective at preventing egg-laying pests from infesting your vegetables. The thicker the fabric, the more frost protection it will provide. But as the thickness increases, the level of light transmitted decreases. Because these fabrics are so light, you can normally drape them right on top of the plants. I prefer to use hoophouses to support the fabric, however, which I'll discuss later.

The third method is to use a cold frame. This is typically a shallow structure with no bottom and a clear or translucent top. Most cold frames are built with wood, but they can be constructed of cinder blocks, hay bales, or anything else that will hold a box shape. If the top is angled toward the sun at about a forty-five-degree angle, you will increase the amount of light reaching the plants. This will also help the rain and snow to slide off. You must be able to open the top so that venting can occur. A cold frame can easily add a month of growing season in the early spring and another month in the fall.

The next method is to build a hoophouse. This is really a portable or temporary greenhouse. I really like hoophouses and have found them to be the easiest and best way to extend your season.

Since all of my gardening is done in raised beds, it's easy to add a hoophouse. For a typical four-foot by eight-foot box, I'll use five supports made out of half-inch plastic electrical conduit. This is the gray tubing that comes in ten-foot lengths, and you can buy it from most hardware or home center stores. Drill three-quarter-inch holes a couple of inches deep into the tops of the boards, equidistant down the eight-foot length. The first and last holes should be in the short boards, but a little inboard so that you do not drill into the screws that are used to attach the boards. Insert the tubing into one hole and bend it over and insert it into the hole on the other side. For a four-foot-wide box, I cut about a foot off the ten-foot length (and always cut the female end off so it will fit in the hole).

You can now cover this structure with a floating row cover if you are looking for just a little protection, or with clear plastic if you want to build a mini-greenhouse. This is an inexpensive way to extend your season, and it's easy to take down during the summer when it is no longer needed. If you use clear plastic, you will need to ventilate it when the sun comes out.

The last method is to build a permanent greenhouse. This is much more expensive and is, well, permanent. There are many good commercial greenhouses available if you want to go that route.

Chapter 7

PLANTS

This section will provide the basic information for the core vegetables that I grow every year in my garden. There are many variables that I look at to see if a vegetable belongs on this core list. The first one is pretty basic. I plant what my family likes to eat. Additionally I plant items that I have reliably grown in the past, that are expensive in the store (usually because they don't ship well), and that are difficult to find organically grown.

Some of the information I present flies in the face of traditional garden lore. What I have found is that many gardening books just keep passing on the same information without regard to scientific fact or, at the very least, some real-world testing. I can only report that these are the practices I have used successfully for many years.

Only in a few cases will I recommend specific varieties of plants. The reason for this is that there are so many different varieties of vegetables today and so many different growing conditions that it's tough to predict what will do best for you. The ones that I do recommend have done very well for me over many years and also have done well for many of my fellow gardeners.

I garden intensively, which means that I grow plants much closer together than most people. I am able to do this because I use a very rich and nutrient-dense soil, and I am also able to give the plants as much water as they need. With average soil and average moisture, you will need to give your plants much more room.

Another key question to answer is, just how many plants do you need? I consistently plant more than I need. The reason is to overcome losses caused by weather, bugs, animals, and raiding relatives, as well as to provide for some local needy families.

ASPARAGUS

Asparagus is a long-lived perennial vegetable that can be productive for twenty or more years if properly cared for. Asparagus is a spring crop and likes cool temperatures and full sun. The part of the plant that is eaten is the spine-like shoots with the scaly tips that emerge from the ground in the spring.

Asparagus is low in calories, contains no cholesterol, and is very low in sodium. It is also a good source of vitamin B6, calcium, magnesium, and zinc. It is a very good source of vitamins A, C, E, and K as well as dietary fiber, protein, thiamine, riboflavin, niacin, folic acid, iron, phosphorus, potassium, copper, manganese, glutathione, and selenium. Wow, that's a mouthful!

Here is what the Michigan Asparagus Advisory Board has to say: "Asparagus is one of the most nutritionally well-balanced vegetables in existence. It leads nearly all produce items in the wide array of nutrients it supplies in significant amounts for a healthy diet."

Soil

Asparagus will grow in most soils as long as it has good drainage. Because of its extensive root system, asparagus will benefit from deeply dug soil amended with all the compost or manure you can spare. It prefers a soil pH level of 6.5 to 7.5. Since this is higher than most plants, you will probably need to add lime.

Planting

Asparagus can be planted from seed, but it is a difficult and time-consuming process. The easiest way to grow it is to plant one-year-old crowns that are healthy and disease-free. A crown is simply the root system of an asparagus plant that was grown from seed.

It really pays to buy crowns of the all-male hybrids since they out yield the traditional Mary Washington varieties by quite a margin. Also, the reason asparagus beds eventually stop doing well is competition from either weeds or the seedlings from the plants themselves. Plant the crowns after the ground has warmed up to at least fifty degrees.

Dig a trench about six inches deep and put in a one-inch layer of compost or well-aged manure. Spread a dusting of rock phosphate or kelp meal on top of this as well. Lay the crowns about eighteen inches apart in rows at least five feet apart. I have some individual ferns that are six feet tall and six feet in diameter, so you need to be very cognizant of that fact when you are planting. Cover the trench with soil (there is no need to gradually do this) and water well.

Watering

Asparagus is very drought-tolerant and requires little additional watering after the first year. The roots will go down as deep as ten feet, and supplemental irrigation is only required in very arid areas.

Weeding

Weeds are the bane of the asparagus plant, especially during the first year or two of crown development. I weed the bed assiduously during the spring and early summer, being careful not to interfere with the crowns or developing ferns.

Fertilizing

Asparagus has an extensive root system and can store a lot of nutrients. After harvest, spread about three inches of compost over the whole bed and add a sprinkling of rock phosphate or kelp meal. The compost will help suppress weeds as well as feed the crowns for next year.

Harvesting

Asparagus spears will start to emerge when the soil temperature reaches fifty degrees. Do not harvest your asparagus the planting year or the year after. The asparagus plant needs to grow and establish a healthy crown, and it will need all of its energy to do that. I will say, however, that I have taken a few spears that second year, and it does not seem to affect the harvest in the ensuing years.

The third year after planting, you only harvest for about the first two weeks. Pick any spear that is about eight inches long, including ones smaller in diameter. Contrary to popular belief, the larger spears are more tender than the smaller ones. This is because the fibrous part of the plant is in the skin; therefore, the larger spears have more of the tender inside flesh.

I like to snap a spear off above the soil surface because this will naturally break it off just above the *woody* section of the plant, eliminating the need for further trimming. Many people cut the spears off just below the soil level, but then they need to cut off the bottom before eating. If the weather is warm, cut every day. If it's cool, go several days between cuttings. You should get about six to ten pickings that first year of harvest.

The second year of harvest you should pick for about four weeks and then the full season every year thereafter (about six to seven weeks).

Maintenance

The green asparagus fern that grows once you stop cutting the spears is very important for next year's crop. The energy from the fern is being transferred down to the crown, and keeping the plants healthy during this period will increase the quantity and quality of next year's spears. This means controlling weeds and pests as well as never cutting or pruning the ferns.

Storing

Asparagus is very perishable and should be harvested in the morning when the air temperature is cool. After picking rinse the spears in cold water, place them in plastic bags, and keep them in the refrigerator. They will keep for a week or two if kept below forty degrees.

Eating

We prefer to eat our asparagus either raw or lightly steamed for three to five minutes. It can also be used in soups or stews, but it does tend to get very soft.

Note: Many people who eat fresh asparagus are able to detect a rather strong odor from their urine. This is caused by sulfur-containing amino acids in the asparagus that break down during digestion. These are the same sulfur compounds that cause skunks to stink. For some unknown reason, not everyone has this issue; but it goes away fairly soon, and there is no known pathological significance.

BEANS

Beans are one of the longest-cultivated plants and have been a significant source of protein throughout history. Beans have high amounts
of fiber, with one cup of cooked beans providing from nine to thirteen
grams of fiber. They are also high in complex carbohydrates, vitamins A
and C, folate, and iron.

Beans are legumes and have bacteria that change nitrogen in the
air to solid forms in the ground. They come in bush varieties and runner
varieties, the latter requiring some sort of support.

There are many different varieties of beans. Whether you're planting snap beans, dry beans, runner beans, soybeans, or lima beans, the
basic instructions are the same. Even better, beans are one of the easiest crops to grow in a home garden.

Soil

Beans will do their best in a rich, well-drained soil. It is beneficial to
loosen the soil at least to a three-inch depth.

Planting

Bean seeds will germinate best if the soil temperature is between sixty
and seventy degrees, which normally occurs one to two weeks after
the last frost date. These seeds hate cold ground, so it does not pay to

push the season too much. The dark-colored seeds will germinate better in cool soil than white seeds will.

Many people say that it is necessary to inoculate your bean seeds, but I have never found that to be the case in my garden. I have tried several test plots and could never see a difference. However, since I fertilize mostly with compost, I probably already have the necessary bacteria in the ground. If you have a new garden, or if you are not sure, then order the correct inoculant with your seeds.

Watering

The key to watering beans is to make sure they have a steady supply of moisture during the time of peak production. They are shallow-rooted plants, so I water every other day during the hot summer.

Weeding

The good news is that beans are one of the easiest crops to keep weeded. This is because they are very fast-growing plants; and if you plant them intensively, they will soon shade the ground and choke out the weeds.

Fertilizing

More good news! I never fertilize beans during the growing season. They do need calcium and phosphorus, but I add those to the soil in the spring along with some compost, which lasts the whole year.

Harvesting

Snap beans should be picked every two or three days during the peak production period. This does two things. First, the constant picking encourages new pod production and dramatically increases the amount of beans that a plant can produce. Second, beans are best eaten when they are young. If the beans enlarge to a size big enough that you can count the seeds, the quality diminishes quickly.

We really like the edible soybean (also known as edamame), a bean that is harvested a little differently. Wait until the seeds are nice and plump but still tender before harvesting them. I pull the whole plant out, hold it upside down, and strip all of the seed pods off.

Storing

Snap beans will store well if they are washed and refrigerated soon after picking. They can also be frozen by blanching them for about two minutes, cooling them in ice water, and then freezing them in a single layer on a cookie sheet. Once they are frozen, put them in a resealable plastic bag so you can remove only the amount you need at a time.

We also like pickled beans. Here is our recipe for *dilly beans*:

Wash beans and wash standard pint jars. Put one dill head, one clove garlic, and up to one-quarter teaspoon ground cayenne pepper (or a couple of whole dried peppers) in each jar. Pack beans in vertically as tight as possible, making sure ends are one-half inch from the top. In a pot, boil one part white vinegar and two parts water and add one-quarter cup pickling salt. Have a water bath kettle hot and ready. Pour boiling salt and vinegar liquid onto beans, leaving one-half inch of headspace. Wipe the rim, add the lid and band, then process for ten minutes. Makes 7 pints. Let set for a couple weeks. Dilly beans are best eaten chilled.

Eating

We like to eat our beans by lightly steaming them for three to five minutes.

BEETS

Beets are one of the most underutilized vegetables in the home garden. Although grown mostly for the roots, the leaves are as good or better than any salad green. Beets are a biennial plant but are typically grown as annuals. They have the highest sugar content of any vegetable.

They are high in folic acid, potassium, calcium, iodine, antioxidants, bioflavonoids, and fiber. The tops contain significantly more iron, vitamin A, potassium, and calcium than the roots. Betacyanin is the phytochemical that gives beets their deep red color, and studies have shown that it can significantly reduce homocysteine levels.

Soil

Beets can be grown in full sun or partial shade and perform best with a soil pH of 6.0 to 6.8. Plant in well-worked soil rich in organic matter. As with all root vegetables, remove all stones and sticks from planting beds so as not to interfere with the growing roots. Make sure to have at least six inches of light soils so that the beets can form nice bulbs.

Planting

Beets are a cool-weather crop and can be planted about three weeks before the last frost date.

Continue planting every three weeks until the middle of summer. Start a fall crop about six weeks before the first frost date.

Beet seeds are a little strange (and technically the seeds are actually fruits) in that there are several seeds together in a cluster. I plant these about one inch deep and an inch apart. When the seedlings are about three inches tall, I thin them to about four inches apart and use the thinnings in salads.

Watering

It is important to keep a consistent level of moisture since the roots can become stunted and tough if the soil is allowed to dry out.

Weeding

Beets don't like competition, so keep the beds weed-free.

Fertilizing

Beets, like all root crops, do better with the right amount of potassium. I add some greensand to my soil amendment mix that I prepare in the fall. Also, beets in particular do very well with the addition of boron. About halfway through the growing season, I'll also add a side dressing of compost.

Harvesting

Beets can be eaten at any size (both the roots and the tops), but the optimum size is about two or three inches in diameter. Given rich soil and plenty of room to grow, beets will grow quite large. I have eaten beets as large as a softball, and they are not woody or tough.

Gently pull the beets from the soil so that you do not break off either the top or the taproot as this will cause bleeding (from the plant, not you!).

Storing

Beets will keep in a plastic bag in the refrigerator for up to three weeks. Unwashed beet greens will keep for three to five days.

Beets will also store well in moist sand at thirty-two degrees for up to four months. In addition, they can be canned or pickled and stored for several years.

Eating

Wash beets under cold running water to remove any dirt or debris. Carefully scrub the beets in order not to bruise them. They can be eaten either raw or cooked. Peeled and grated beets are a wonderful addition to a salad.

BROCCOLI

Broccoli has been maligned by kids and presidents, but it is a flavorful and very nutritious green vegetable.

There are many health benefits associated with broccoli. It provides vitamins B1 (thiamine), B2 (riboflavin), B3 (niacin), B5 (pantothenic acid), B6, B9 (folate), A , C, and K. It contains the minerals calcium, magnesium, phosphorus, and potassium and has a high fiber content.

And it gets even better. Scientists from Oregon State University say they've found cancer-fighting agents in broccoli that selectively target and kill diseased cells while leaving normal cells healthy.

Broccoli is one of the most popular vegetables of the brassica (also called cruciferous) family. It is a cool-weather crop usually grown in the spring and fall. I prefer the fall planting when the heads are able to de-velop while the days are still warm and the nights are cold.

Soil

Broccoli likes a sunny site and fertile, well-drained soil. It is a heavy feeder, so add in several inches of compost or organic fertilizer before transplanting.

Planting

For the earliest harvest, start seeds indoors six weeks before the last spring frost, and set out the young plants when they're about four

43

weeks old. For a fall harvest, start seeds about eight weeks before your first fall frost, and set out the plants when they're four weeks old. Space the plants about sixteen inches apart.

Watering

Keep the soil moist but not waterlogged.

Weeding

I plant broccoli through the black landscape fabric, so I don't do any weeding. Broccoli, however, can tolerate more weeds than other vegetables.

Fertilizing

I like to add a small band of organic fertilizer around each plant right when the flower heads are starting to form.

Harvesting

Harvest when the buds of the head are firm and tight, cutting five to ten inches down on the stalk. Don't make the mistake of thinking that this is the end of the harvest. For about six weeks after you cut off the central head, an abundance of side shoots will grow and often exceed the total of that first crop. Continuously remove these shoots to ensure that the plant will keep producing.

Storing

As soon as I pick the broccoli, I spray some hydrogen peroxide (or you may use vinegar) on it and wash it under a hard stream of cold water. This will remove any bugs or dirt that can hide in the tight clusters. Broccoli can be stored in the refrigerator for a couple of weeks, but any excess harvest should be frozen, pickled, or canned.

I much prefer the freezer method. Blanch the heads for about three minutes in boiling water, and then stop the cooking process by submersing the heads in ice water for the same amount of time. Dry them on a towel and then place them in freezer bags or vacuum seal them. They will keep fine for at least a year.

Eating

Broccoli is very good raw, although not a lot of people eat it that way. Our favorite way to eat it raw is dipped in some homemade hummus. Lightly steamed broccoli with a little butter tastes great. For a unique taste treat, try putting a little nutritional yeast on the broccoli to give it a bit of a cheesy taste and texture.

BRUSSELS SPROUTS

Brussels sprouts are a slow-growing, long-season vegetable that look like miniature cabbages growing on a stalk. They are part of the brassica family, which includes cabbage, collard greens, broccoli, kale, and kohlrabi.

There are hundreds of medical studies that are focused on Brussels sprouts, and over half of those studies involve the health benefits of this cruciferous vegetable in relationship to cancer. Brussels sprouts are thought to be native to Belgium, specifically to a region near its capital, Brussels, after which they are named.

Brussels sprouts are an excellent source of vitamins C and K. They are a very good source of folate, vitamin A, manganese, dietary fiber, potassium, vitamin B6, and thiamine (vitamin B1).

Sprouts can be a bit difficult to grow because of their climatic requirements. They prefer cool weather and are at their best when they mature during sunny days and frosty nights. They cannot take a hard freeze, however, so there is a thin line between a perfect harvest and a frozen one.

Soil

You will want to plant Brussels sprouts in soil that is rich in organic matter for both the nutrient value and the moisture-holding abilities. They like a sweet soil with a pH of about 6.5.

Planting

I start my plants indoors about two weeks before the last frost. I transplant them to the garden when they are about four weeks old and plant about eighteen inches apart.

Watering

Brussels sprouts like plentiful and consistent moisture. They are shallow-rooted and need to be watered every other day during the hot summer months.

Weeding

I have found that sprouts grow best when I plant them through landscape fabric. If you are unable to do that, I recommend hand weeding so as not to disturb the shallow roots. You should also top dress them with about an inch of compost when the plants are six to eight inches tall.

Fertilizing

Brussels sprouts are a heavy feeder, especially of nitrogen. I will add an inch or so of compost to the bed (right on top of the landscape fabric), and then I'll side dress the rows every three to four weeks with some blood meal and a little borax (for the boron) and Epsom salts (for the magnesium).

Harvesting

There are two schools of thought for harvesting Brussels sprouts. The first is by cutting off the growing tip when the bottom sprout is about the size of your thumb. This will cause the energy of the plant to fill out the existing sprouts and you can harvest the whole stalk when the individual sprouts are about one to one and one-half inches in diameter.

In the second method, you just start harvesting from the bottom of the stalk when the sprouts have reached their desired size.

I typically end up utilizing both methods. At the beginning of the harvest season, I like to pick some of the early sprouts just because I can't wait. I then wait for the first few frosts and then harvest the entire stalk.

Storing

There are three ways we store Brussels sprouts. First, you can pick the individual sprouts, removing any yellow or damaged leaves, and store them in your refrigerator. They will keep for a week or maybe two. The second method is to cut off the entire stalk just below the first sprouts and store it in a cool and dry place for up to one month. Last, you can blanch the individual sprouts for a couple of minutes, followed by an icy water bath and freezing them in a single layer on a cookie sheet. Put them in a freezer bag after about an hour in the freezer, and they will store this way for about a year.

Eating

As with all of the cruciferous vegetables, be sure not to overcook Brussels sprouts. Not only do you lose many of the nutrients, but they can emit an unpleasant sulfur smell.

We like our sprouts either lightly steamed or sautéed. After cutting off any yellow or damaged leaves, put the sprouts in your steamer and cook for approximately five minutes or until they turn bright green and are tender when pierced with a fork.

But our favorite way to prepare sprouts is to stir-fry them. We cut them into halves or quarters and sauté them with cut-up garlic and onion in coconut oil. Cook about five minutes or until they reach the desired level.

CABBAGE

Cabbage belongs to the cole crop family (brassica), which includes broccoli, Brussels sprouts, cauliflower, collards, kale, and kohlrabi.

In the middle ages, cabbage was called the *drug of the poor* because of its medicinal qualities. There have been many studies that show eating cabbage reduces the risk of colon and other cancers.

Cabbage is also an excellent source of vitamin C (actually more than oranges), beta carotene, and folic acid as well as a large number of minerals, including iodine, sulfur, calcium, magnesium, and potassium. Cabbage is high in fiber but low in calories, with one cup amounting to only fifteen calories. And finally, it stores longer than any other green leafy vegetable.

We like both red and green cabbages and use the storage varieties for sauerkraut.

Soil

Cabbage likes a sunny site (although it will tolerate partial shade) and fertile, well-drained soil. It is a heavy feeder, so add in several inches of compost or organic fertilizer before transplanting.

Planting

Cabbage is a cool-weather crop and therefore does best in the spring and fall. For the earliest harvest, start seeds indoors four to six weeks before the last spring frost, and set out the young plants when they're about four weeks old. You can also direct seed in the late spring; and the seedlings can withstand a light frost, although these will not do as well since they will be maturing during the heat of the summer. For a fall harvest, start seeds about eight weeks before your first fall frost, and set out the plants when they're four weeks old. Space the plants about sixteen inches apart.

Good companion plants are onions, garlic, peas, potatoes, and herbs.

Watering

Keep the soil moist but not waterlogged. Mulching helps to keep the moisture consistent so that the heads do not split.

Weeding

I plant cabbage through landscape fabric, so I don't do any weeding. It does have a rather shallow root system, so hand weed close to the plants.

Fertilizing

I apply a band of organic fertilizer several weeks after transplanting, making sure it contains boron, calcium, and magnesium. Cabbage is rather finicky about fertility, though, and excessive fertilizing can cause the heads to split.

Harvesting

Harvest cabbage as soon as the heads are firm to the touch by cutting the cabbage head from the stem. If you cut the plant just below the head and above the big lower leaves, you can also harvest the small heads that appear on the stem a few weeks later. They are best when they are small—about two or three inches in diameter. Spring cabbage is best when harvested at about softball size, when the heads are both tasty and tender. As the summer approaches, they will tend to grow quite fast.

Storing

As soon as I pick cabbage, I spray some hydrogen peroxide (or vinegar) on it and wash it under a hard stream of cold water to remove any dirt or bugs. The key to the proper storage of cabbage is to keep it cold and keep it wrapped. If you don't like plastic wrap, you can use Tupperware or Pyrex containers, making sure to match the container size to the head. The cabbage will store for several months like this, and my experience is that the red varieties store longer than the green ones.

Our favorite way to store (and eat) cabbage is to turn it into sauerkraut.

<u>Eating</u>

Cabbage is another vegetable that is very good raw and just cut up in a salad, and there are many good coleslaw recipes out there. Cabbage soup is one of my all-time favorites, and my Polish grandmother always made stuffed cabbage called *golabki*.

CARROTS

Carrots are a big nutritional storehouse, providing an excellent source of vitamins A, B6, and C. In addition they contain potassium, thiamine, folic acid, and magnesium as well as a form of calcium easily absorbed by the body. No other vegetable or fruit contains as much of the potent antioxidant carotene as carrots. This is a truly versatile vegetable, which also contains a pectin fiber that has been found to have cholesterol-lowering properties.

Since carrots are a biennial, they spend the whole first year storing up nutrients in anticipation of making seeds the second year. Of course, most of us sneak in and harvest those storehouses before they can even think of reproducing...

Soil

There are two secrets to growing good carrots, and they both relate to the soil. First, carrots need a rich, sandy soil with good compost content (but not too rich or they will form lush green tops with no roots) and a pH of 5.8 to 6.8. Second, this soil needs to be at least twelve inches deep and must be free of all stones, twigs, and other debris to prevent interference with the growing roots. As with other root crops, I add some wood ashes at the time of planting to provide the necessary potassium.

Planting

Choose a spot in full sun as carrots don't do nearly as well with any shade. Sow carrots about three weeks before the last expected frost. I use the pelleted variety so that I can more accurately control the number of plants. Thin the bed so that there are three to four inches between plants, depending on the variety. I pull the carrots very gently from the ground and eat them as baby carrots.

Watering

Carrots require a steady supply of moisture to the subsoil, and this means fairly frequent and deep watering. Since carrots do best when they mature quickly, a deep, rich soil and constant moisture will result in a fast-growing crop.

Weeding

Carrots are one of the toughest vegetables to keep weed-free. I usually don't add any organic mulch until the plants have been thinned to at least two inches apart. The problem is that when I pull the weeds, I end up pulling the little carrots as well. The only way I've found to beat this is to weed the beds every few days, getting the weeds when they are very small.

Fertilizing

I do not apply any additional fertilizer during the growing season. Too much fertilizer (especially nitrogen) will cause big green tops but small roots or too many forked roots.

Harvesting

Carrots can be harvested at any stage after they turn orange. I like to grab the carrot by the top of the root and wiggle it in a circular motion to break the suction with the ground and then pull straight up. This method causes the least disruption to the neighboring plants. It isn't necessary to harvest the whole crop at once—just pick as needed.

Storing

Carrots are a wonderful vegetable to store. They can stay in the ground until it freezes and, if covered with a good layer of leaves or mulch, they will store the entire winter. I have had good success storing them in buried five-gallon buckets (under a bale of hay) and also in moist sand in the root cellar.

Eating

Carrots are a very versatile vegetable, eaten raw, grated for coleslaw, or cooked in soups and stews. They are wonderful sautéed in a little olive or coconut oil.

CELERY

Although celery is not a very nutritionally dense vegetable, it does have a lot to offer. First, it is very low in calories—about 6 calories in the average stalk. It is said that celery is the only negative-calorie vegetable because you will burn more than six calories eating a stalk. About 95 percent of celery is water, with about 2 percent fiber, 2 percent carbohydrates, and 1 percent protein. The celery leaves are also quite nutritious and tasty and are wonderful in soups and stews.

Celery has vitamins A and C, iron, calcium, potassium, phosphorus, and folate. It also contains compounds called phthalides that are thought to reduce blood pressure.

Celery has been used for medicinal purposes in the Mediterranean. It is not commonly found in the home garden because it is somewhat difficult to grow. But once you have mastered the requirements, celery is a very rewarding crop; and the taste and texture of homegrown celery are much better than anything you can buy in the store. Celery is one of the *Dirty Dozen* (see appendix B), and organic celery can be difficult to find.

Celery requires a very long growing season (usually about five months), likes lots of water and nutrients, and prefers cooler weather.

Soil

This is one area that you can definitely not skimp on. Celery is a very heavy feeder, and I literally plant my celery in a raised bed with about two feet of pure aged compost. You could probably get by with less and some topsoil mixed in, but this is what I have found works best for me. If you are not able to do this, I used to dig a trench about eighteen inches deep in the garden and fill it with aged compost. The plants won't get quite as big but will still be very edible. I also add a handful of crushed eggshells to the bottom of the hole when I plant.

Planting

Celery needs to be started indoors at least ten weeks before the last frost of the season. The seeds are tiny, and they take about two to three weeks to germinate. Growth is rather slow, and you will need to be diligent about transplanting to bigger containers so that the plants do not become root-bound. They can take a light frost if they have been hardened off outside during the day, so I plant them outside about two weeks before the last frost in rows about twelve inches apart.

Watering

Probably the most difficult thing about growing good celery is that it requires a steady and plentiful supply of water, especially during the hot summer months. One big advantage to planting in pure compost is that it retains moisture better than any other soil. I water about one inch every other day.

Weeding

Weeds are not particularly bothersome for celery, but I do plant it through landscape fabric to ease the weeding burden.

Fertilizing

I either side dress with my organic fertilizer about every three weeks during the season or alternate with a foliar feeding of fish emulsion or compost tea.

Harvesting

You can pick celery at almost any size. I use a sharp knife and just cut the number of stalks that I need, starting from the larger outer ones and working my way inward. Some people blanch the stalks by hilling up dirt or making a little tent. I prefer the dark green color and more intense flavor, so I avoid that whole step. The other trick is to plant the individual plants close together

Storing

I have found that the best way to store celery is to wash it in cold water, air dry for a few minutes, and then completely wrap it in aluminum foil. It will stay fresh for up to three weeks in the vegetable bin of your refrigerator.

Although this vegetable is most often eaten fresh, we dry a couple of dozen stalks each year to use in soups and stews during the winter. Here is the process I use:

- Wash and dry as you normally would.

- Slice the stalks as thin as you can (I use a mandoline, and the slices end up being a little less than one-eighth inch thick).

- Spread them in a single layer in your dehydrator and dry for eight to ten hours or until they are light and crispy (there is no need to blanch).

- We also dry the leaves for about six hours at the lowest temperature.

- Store in an airtight container and add directly to soups and stews. (You can also grind the celery and mix with salt to use as a seasoned salt.)

Eating

You will find that fresh, homegrown celery has a much more intense flavor than store-bought. We like to eat it raw or cooked lightly in stir-fries, and the leaves add a great flavor to soups and stews.

CORN

There are two distinct types of corn: sweet corn and field (or dent) corn. Sweet corn is harvested and eaten before the kernels mature and only represents about 1 percent of the corn grown in the United States.

Almost all of the corn you see growing on huge farms today is field corn. It is picked when the kernels are dry and hard. At this stage the corn is unfit for human consumption. It is used primarily to feed animals and is also turned into other products, such as high-fructose corn syrup and ethanol.

Humans have grown and eaten corn for thousands of years. Corn has gotten a bad rap lately, and some of it is justified. Part of the problem is that big agribusiness in this country grows mostly GMO or genetically modified corn and then mutilates it to turn it into another form. Corn has a high starch and calorie content but is fairly low in protein. Most field corn has about 9 percent protein, but some of the newer Indian corn varieties have as much as 15 percent. Finally, corn requires more fertility and water than most other crops.

Most home gardeners are only interested in growing sweet corn. I agree that it is tough to beat the taste of a freshly picked ear of corn. There are also new hybrids of sweet and supersweet corn available. But there are several subsets of field corn to consider growing in your home garden.

Flint corn (often called Indian corn) is a type of field corn that is very edible for humans. Popcorn is an example of this type. Another field corn is flour corn, which is most commonly used to make tortillas.

Soil

Corn thrives best in deep, rich, easily worked soil. It does well in a wide range of pH levels, with 6.0 to 6.5 providing optimum results.

Planting

Most varieties of corn require a warm soil temperature of about sixty degrees to germinate. Plant the kernels about one inch deep and nine inches apart. If you have very fertile soil, the rows can be as close as one foot apart. You will get better pollination if you plant the corn in blocks rather than in long rows.

I have found that skip planting (reseeding the areas where germination did not occur) does not work well for corn. The earlier-germinating plants tend to shade out the newer ones, and they do not pollinate at the same time. What I do is plant a bunch of kernels in an area off to the side and use these seedlings to transplant into the openings in the rows.

Since corn is wind-pollinated, you should isolate your corn from other varieties that are pollinating at the same time. I have found that it takes at least one hundred yards of distance to accomplish this.

Watering

To get the best yields, provide about one and one-half to two inches of water per week. Corn is very fast-growing and it needs a lot of moisture.

Weeding

Corn is a shallow-rooted plant, and you must take care not to injure those roots while you are removing the weeds. I use a sharp hoe to slice off the weeds just below ground level.

Fertilizing

Corn is a heavy feeder and is one of the few vegetables that needs high amounts of nitrogen. I rake in my standard fertilizer mix before planting, but then I side dress the plants with blood meal when they are about a foot tall and again about a week after the tassels first appear. I apply about a pound of 12 percent nitrogen blood meal per hundred lineal feet of row.

Harvesting

It is important to harvest sweet corn at just the right maturity (and actually you are picking it in its green state). This generally occurs about three weeks from the time the ears develops their silks. The unhusked ears should feel firm, with full kernels at the tip and dry, brown silks. If you pierce a kernel with your fingernail, a milky liquid should squirt out. If the corn is not ripe yet, it will ooze out a watery liquid. If it is overripe, the kernel will be tough with only a little liquid.

There is a technique to picking corn, and it's all in the wrist action. If you hold the main stem with one hand, grab the ear with the other, and then bend the ear down sharply while twisting, it should break cleanly from the plant.

Flour and parching corns should be left to dry on the plant and then shucked. Parching corn is a variety of flour corn and is similar to popcorn. When heated they expand slightly instead of exploding like popcorn and are much sweeter.

Storing

The best way to eat sweet corn is as soon as possible after picking. I like to tell the story of the time I took a propane stove out to the corn patch and put a pot of water on it to boil. I then peeled the leaves off the plant and bent the whole thing over until the ear was in the boiling water. You can't get any fresher than that!

If you do need to store the sweet corn, keep it as cold as possible but above freezing.

For long-term storage of sweet corn, I usually blanch it for just two minutes, cut it off the cob and then freeze it. If you dry the ears and vacuum seal the bags, they will last for at least a year in the freezer. I have also dehydrated corn and then vacuum sealed the bag, and it will store this way for years.

Eating

I like to eat sweet corn raw, but most people cook it by boiling it for three to five minutes. It is also good grilled in the husk after soaking it in cold water.

The flour corns can be used for bread, cakes, and tortillas. The parching corns are wonderful when cooked by heating them in a hot skillet until they expand.

CUCUMBER

The cucumber is one of our oldest cultivated crops. It is a member of the cucurbit family and is related to squash and melons. Cucumbers are a good source of vitamins A, C, and K. They also are high in potassium, very low in calories, and contain no fat or cholesterol. Some people claim that cucumbers are particularly beneficial to our hair, skin, and nails. It is also said that they can aid in digestion and prevent constipation.

There are two basic types of cucumbers: slicing and pickling. The slicers are generally larger, with smooth skins. The pickling ones are bred to—yes, you guessed it—be turned into pickles.

Soil

Like other members of the squash family, cucumbers grow best in a rich, friable soil with lots of organic matter. They are a hearty plant type and will tolerate a fairly wide range of soil conditions.

Planting

Cucumbers like warm soil, so it generally pays to wait until the soil warms up to the seventy-degree range. I typically direct seed cucumbers in the garden, although you can get a head start by sowing seeds indoors about two weeks before the last frost date.

I have found that the best way to grow cucumbers is up a string or trellis, planted in a row. The plants will easily get six to eight feet high, and growing them vertically keeps the cucumbers straight and easier to find and pick. I plant most varieties about eight inches apart.

Watering

Like any vegetable with a high water content, cucumbers need plenty of water to achieve that. A deep watering twice a week during the hot summer months should do the trick.

Weeding

I grow cucumbers through black plastic mulch since this is a heat-loving plant. If you grow them in bare soil, be careful when weeding since cucumbers have a shallow root system.

Fertilizing

Cucumbers are not heavy feeders, so the only thing I do during the season is to side dress the rows with a little of my organic fertilizer mix when the vines really start to flower profusely.

Harvesting

The real secret to picking cumbers is to do it sooner rather than later. The larger the fruit, the more likely that it will have little taste or even become bitter. If they start turning yellow, you have waited too long. Also, frequent picking will cause the plant to keep producing.

I have found that if I cut the stem about one-quarter inch above the fruit, the cucumbers will store longer.

Eating

We eat most of our cucumbers cut up in a traditional salad. But during the high production periods of late summer, we make cucumber salads with homemade yogurt and fresh onions and dill.

GARLIC

Garlic's health benefits and medicinal qualities are well documented. Garlic is a powerful antibiotic and antioxidant and has a long history of assisting with lowering blood pressure and cholesterol. China is the leading grower of garlic in the world, and they saw widespread shortages in 2009 as the Chinese believe that it can prevent swine flu.

Garlic is a member of the allium family, which also includes leeks, shallots, and onions. It is relatively easy to grow, and the individual cloves act as seeds so it is a self-sustaining crop. It interacts well with most other vegetables and flowers.

Soil

Garlic will grow well in most soils but really appreciates a deeply dug sandy loam bed with a generous amount of organic matter. It has a fairly deep root system, so it is beneficial to dig to a depth of six to twelve inches. The soil should drain well, as the garlic bulbs can rot if they get too wet. Garlic does best in full sun and with a pH of 6.2 to 6.8.

Preparation for Planting

Shortly before planting, break apart the bulbs to separate the individual cloves. (This is called *cracking*.) Depending on the variety, each bulb has five to fifteen cloves. I segregate the cloves into two piles: big and small. We will eat or preserve the small cloves within a short amount of time, and I will plant the big cloves. The largest cloves produce the biggest bulbs, so it really pays to go through this process. If you find that you have too many small cloves, you can also plant them for spring baby garlic. Just plant these small bulbs very close together (one to two inches apart) and pick them when they are twelve to sixteen inches tall. They will look like scallions, but the taste is all garlic.

Planting

Garlic needs some exposure to freezing temperatures, so most people plant in the late fall or perhaps the very early spring. The bulbs like some warmth after planting to develop a nice root system before the ground freezes. The ideal time is four to six weeks before the ground freezes. I usually plant my garlic right around Halloween every year. Don't worry if you get some green shoots coming up before winter—the garlic will do just fine. The bulbs should be planted with the top (or pointed side) up and covered with about two inches of soil. In fertile soil you can plant them about four to six inches apart in rows about eight inches apart. If you have severe winters, mulching can help prevent ground heaving and ensure a more constant temperature and moisture level. I remove the mulch in the early spring to help the soil warm quicker.

Watering

Garlic likes to have abundant moisture during the growing season. There should never be standing water, but the plants should never dry out either. Make sure the soil is well watered after planting right up until the ground freezes. Keep the plants well irrigated until about four weeks before you harvest them (the scapes or flower stems should be standing high at this point), and then stop all watering. This will reduce the chances of rot forming and will encourage development of the papery covering that protects the cloves during storage.

Weeding

If you want nice garlic, you must be very dedicated to your weeding. Garlic hates competition, so keep your beds as weeded as possible.

Fertilizing

Garlic is a heavy feeder and appreciates a constant supply of nutrients. If you dug in a few inches of compost before you planted, then most of your fertilizer is already in the ground. I generally side dress the plants at the end of April with some of my organic fertilizer and then do a foliar feeding of kelp and fish emulsion a month or so later.

Scapes

There seems to be some controversy on whether or not you should cut the scapes, which usually occur only on the hardneck varieties. I have found that you will get slightly bigger bulbs if you cut off the scapes before they mature. But the biggest reason to cut these off is that they are absolutely delicious pan-fried in a little oil or butter. Just be sure to cut them when they are young (generally when they turn and head back down toward the ground, but before they do a full 360 degrees).

Harvesting

Many garlic growers do very well—until it comes time to harvest. Everyone seems to have a different idea as to the optimum time to harvest, but it really depends on what you want to do with your cloves. If your goal is to store them for the winter, you will need to pick them earlier—when the tops are upright and showing about half green. This allows for the best formation of the protective papery wrapping. If you intend on eating them within a month or so, you can leave them in the ground until the plants turn brown but harvest before they fall over. If you leave them in too long, you run the risk of the cloves splitting or rotting. Do not pull on the stem to pick the plant. Use a pitchfork to loosen the ground around it, and pull the plant out by the bulb. Garlic has an extensive root system, and you must take care not to break the stalk. Do not let the plants lie in the sun for any length of time before they are cured, as this can affect the flavor.

Curing

If you plan on storing your garlic, you need to properly cure it. The entire plant should be hung up in a dry, well-ventilated area for two or three weeks. I tie up about a dozen plants at a time, and hang them up in the woodshed. Do not wash the plants, but you may want to brush off some of the excess soil. After curing, cut off the roots and the stalk about an inch from the base.

Storing

Garlic should be stored at a constant temperature of fifty to sixty degrees in a well-ventilated area. It will last up to six months if it was properly cured.

I also thinly slice some of the cloves and dehydrate them. They will store great this way for several years, making it easy to incorporate them into soups and stews.

Garlic is also easy to store by pickling it, and I use a recipe almost identical to the one for dilly beans.

Eating

We eat most of our garlic fresh in salads and dips, but it is also a staple in many cooked recipes.

Varieties

The variety that I have grown for many years is Siberian. It is a purple-striped garlic, typically with six very large cloves and a creamy white inside. It packs lots of heat!

KALE

Kale is a fast-growing, green leafy vegetable similar to collards and Swiss chard. It grows best in cool weather. Part of the brassica family, kale can be eaten raw or cooked in soups, stews, and stir-fries. It is very hardy and will grow well into winter. Kale is rich in vitamins A, C, and K and is high in potassium, calcium, and iron. It is also a good source of fiber. Kale is a rich source of organosulfur compounds, which have been shown to reduce the risk of many cancers, including colon cancer. Recent research indicates that the phytonutrients in kale work to increase production of enzymes involved in detoxification.

Kale is my family's most important vegetable crop. It is very nutrient-dense and easy to grow. It also has the longest harvesting season of any vegetable we plant. We eat fresh kale from the garden virtually year-round.

Soil

Kale prefers a fertile, well-drained soil high in organic matter and with a pH of 6.0 to 7.0. Although full sun is needed in the spring and fall, partial shade works well in the hot summer months. Mulching during the hot months is important to keep the soil cool.

Planting

Kale can be planted as soon as the ground can be worked. Sow the seeds one-quarter to one-half inch deep, one inch apart in rows about eighteen inches apart. Thin seedlings to twelve inches apart. (I eat or transplant the thinnings.) For earlier harvests, start the seedlings indoors and transplant into the garden about four to six weeks before the last spring frost. Kale will grow three to four feet tall, so make sure you have enough headroom if you are growing it in a cold frame or hoophouse.

Watering

Consistent watering of about an inch per week during the growing season is the key to good kale. It can withstand dry conditions, but the leaves tend to get bitter tasting.

Weeding

Kale is one of the least demanding vegetables I grow and seems unaffected by weeds.

Fertilizing

Since you are growing kale for the foliage, a good supply of nitrogen is beneficial. Side dressing with compost or feeding with fish emulsion throughout the growing season will keep your kale vigorous and sweet.

Harvesting

Kale can be harvested at any time during the growing season. The young, small leaves have a light, sweet taste and are great in salads. The older leaves are more pungent and are good cooked. Harvest the whole plant or cut off the outer leaves and let the central stalk continue to grow and produce more leaves.

Storing

Kale can be stored in the refrigerator for up to a week. I have also successfully frozen kale. Wash it thoroughly, blanch it for two minutes, rinse it in cold water, put it in a Ziploc bag (or vacuum seal), and put it in the freezer. It will store well for about a year.

Eating

Although raw kale is a bit tough, we like to finely chop it and add it to a traditional salad. It also makes a nice veggie roll-up wrap. Kale can be sautéed in a little oil with some onions and garlic for a nice side dish. Kale soup is a staple in our house during the winter, where we use blanched and frozen kale. Also, kale chips are a very healthy alternative to store-bought potato chips. My wife has a green smoothie drink every morning with the main ingredient being kale.

Varieties

The perennial favorite that I grow is Winterbor. It is the hardiest of all kales that I have tried and provides a steady harvest of deeply curled, blue-green leaves. Redbor is a purple-red version of Winterbor that is a little milder. This is often sold as an ornamental plant but we have found it to be very edible.

KOHLRABI

Kohlrabi, which is grown mainly for its swollen, bulbous stem, is a cross between a turnip and a cabbage. (In German *kohl* means cabbage and *rabi* means turnip.) It is very easy to grow and nutritious, too. Kohlrabi contains chromium, potassium, magnesium, phosphorus, and vitamins C and B6 as well as being a good source of dietary fiber.

Kohlrabi can be eaten raw or cooked. The flavor is similar to that of a mild white turnip, with hints of celery and a bit of nuttiness as well. The young leaves can be eaten raw or steamed like spinach. It is one of the hardiest of all garden vegetables and can be harvested well into the fall and early winter. Like other cole crops, kohlrabi does best in cool weather, but it can tolerate warm weather better than most other brassicas. It is very popular in Europe, but it is not very big in most of the United States.

Soil

Kohlrabi will grow in most soils; but since it is such a fast grower, it does best with a high level of compost or manure in a well-drained soil. The root system is fairly shallow so it does not require deep tilling. Plant in full sun, and the pH should be between 6.3 and 6.8.

Planting

Kohlrabi can be direct seeded outdoors about three to four weeks before the last spring frost. If you would like an earlier harvest, you may start the seeds indoors and transplant about two weeks before the last frost. Sow seeds thinly one-quarter to one-half inch deep in rows about a foot apart. Thin seedlings to eight inches apart. For a fall crop, directly sow seeds into the garden in late summer.

Watering

I recommend at least an inch of water per week. If the plants do not receive enough water, the texture will become woody and the taste will become bitter.

Weeding

As with any other shallow-rooted vegetable, kohlrabi does best with little competition from weeds. Take care not to interfere with the roots or break the stem below the bulb.

Fertilizing

If you have amended your soil with several inches of compost before planting, very little additional fertilizer is required. A side dressing of organic fertilizer or some manure tea about a month after planting is all that is needed. Kohlrabi is a fast-growing vegetable, so the initial soil fertility is the key.

Harvesting

Kohlrabi can be harvested anytime after the bulbs form, but most varieties are at their best at about three inches in diameter. The Kossak storage variety is best picked at about eight inches in diameter. Most plants mature in about fifty days.

Storing

Kohlrabi can be stored for several weeks in the refrigerator if you remove the leaves and stems and place the individual bulbs in sealed plastic bags. They will also keep for one to two months in a cold, moist environment.

To freeze kohlrabi, peel and cut into pieces. Blanch for two minutes and chill in ice water. Drain and spread on a tray in a single layer and freeze for one hour. Put the frozen pieces in plastic bags or vacuum pack them. Frozen kohlrabi will keep for up to six months.

Eating

Virtually all of the kohlrabi we eat is raw. Chill the whole bulb in the refrigerator, thinly slice, and add a little sea salt for a crunchy and delectable treat.

LETTUCE

Lettuce is a wonderful vegetable to grow. Most people like it, it does not take much space, it is easy to grow, and you can enjoy multiple harvests during the growing season. It also offers a nice mix of nutrients, including beta carotene, calcium, iron, folate, and vitamins A , C, and K. Generally the darker the greens the more nutrition there is.

Most varieties of lettuce prefer cooler weather and tend to bolt (or go to seed) in the hot summer sun.

Soil

Lettuce, like most other leafy green vegetables, prefers a nice sandy loam with a lot of compost mixed in. It will grow in just about any soil, if not as vigorously.

Planting

Most gardeners direct seed their lettuce in early to mid-spring. I like to start mine indoors in small soil blocks to ensure that I transplant the strongest seedlings and completely fill up a raised bed. I only do this for the first planting in the spring, however. After that they get direct seeded in succession about every ten days. I plant the loose-leaf varieties about four inches apart. Since our summers tend to be fairly moderate, I can usually continue this planting well into the fall.

Occasionally the lettuce will turn bitter from the heat, and I turn these heads into compost.

Watering

Lettuce is a shallow-rooted plant and needs a consistent supply of moisture at the top layer of soil. This typically means watering every other day during the middle of summer.

Weeding

Lettuce grows so quickly that weeding is generally not an issue. I tend to keep the bed well weeded to prevent eating weeds I might inadvertently harvest with the lettuce.

Fertilizing

If you were able to mix in a good amount of compost before the growing season, then you probably don't need any additional nutrients. If not you may want to do a foliar feeding of fish emulsion when the plants are about three or four inches tall.

Harvesting

Lettuce can be harvested at any stage. I like to use a sharp knife or a pair of scissors to cut off the plants about an inch above ground level. Most varieties will send out new leaves and can be harvested several times.

Storing

Lettuce can be stored unwashed in the refrigerator for up to one month.

Eating

Lettuce is a *just-in-time* vegetable, and we tend to only pick it right before mealtime.

ONIONS

Since onions are one of my core vegetables, I strive to grow enough to last us all year. They can be eaten raw or cooked and add a lot of flavor to many dishes.

Onions are fat- and cholesterol-free, very low in sodium, high in vitamin C, and a good source of fiber and other key nutrients. They also contain the flavonoid called quercetin, which has been shown in studies to protect against cardiovascular disease and cancer; and organosulfur compounds, which have been linked to lowering blood pressure and cholesterol.

There are two different types of onions: *long-day onions* and *short-day onions*. Long-day onions do better in the northern states and need about fifteen to sixteen hours of sunlight to mature properly. Short-day onions work well in the southern states and need about twelve hours of sunlight to produce bulbs.

The secret to growing great onions is to get nice, big, dark-green tops before the bulbs form. The size of the final bulb is determined by the number and size of green leaves at the time the bulb starts to form. For each green leaf, there will be a ring of the onion. The larger the leaf, the larger the ring will be.

Soil

The best soil for onions has lots of organic matter incorporated into it and a neutral pH. Strong-tasting onions have probably been grown in soil that is too acidic.

Planting

Onions can be grown from seeds, transplants, or sets. Transplants look like miniature green onions, and sets are small onion bulbs.

- *From seeds:* Plant seeds about three-eighths inch deep and about an inch apart. Once seedlings emerge, thin to about every four inches.

- *From transplants:* This is my favorite way to grow onions. Plant the transplants one inch deep and space them about four inches apart. On the sweet varieties, I plant them every two inches and pick every other one to use as green onions.

- *From sets:* Planting sets is the easiest way to grow bulb onions. It decreases harvest time, too, since they are *started* onions. Plant sets about one and one-half to two inches deep and four inches apart.

Watering

Onions need a lot of water when they are rooting and developing the tops. I deeply water every other day during the hot summer months. When the bulbs start to form, cut back on the watering.

Weeding

Onions do not like any competition from weeds, and I am much pickier about weeding onions than most other crops. Planting onions intensively, as I do, requires hand weeding.

Fertilizing

Onions like a high amount of phosphorus when they are at the rooting stage and a high level of nitrogen for the rest of the growing season. I incorporate a band of rock phosphate in a trench about three or four inches deep in the row where the transplanted onions will go. I add a little of my fertilizer mix every three weeks until the tops start to turn soft, and then I stop all fertilization.

Harvesting

Onions can be harvested at any stage. The plants thinned from a row can be used as green onions. However, onion bulbs are ready when about half the tops have fallen over and the bulbs' skins have a papery feel. I then gently flatten the rest of the tops, being careful not to break any. A few days later, I'll dig all of the bulbs up, gently brush off any loose soil, and cure them in a warm, dry place out of the sun. After the onions are fully cured (about two to four weeks depending on temperature and humidity), I cut off the dried top and the roots.

Storing

Onions should be stored in a cool, dry location, with about forty degrees being ideal. Do not allow them to freeze, or they will turn to mush. The key is to give them lots of air circulation. I hang mine in the fruit cellar in mesh bags.

Eating

It's amazing how many meals we eat that have onions in them. Onions are standard in all of our fresh salads and a core ingredient in soups, stews, omelets, and sandwiches.

PEPPERS

Peppers have the widest range of colors and flavors of any vegetable. They do best in areas with long and warm summers. I have found that the smaller and hotter the pepper, the easier it is to grow. Green peppers are immature fruit; and the taste, texture, and nutrient value will improve dramatically if you let them mature. Most varieties will turn red when they fully ripen.

Sweet bell peppers contain high amounts of vitamins A and C and good amounts of vitamin B6, folate, and magnesium.

Peppers belong to the nightshade family and are very similar in their growing requirements to tomatoes.

Soil

Peppers prefer soil that is neutral pH, rich in organic matter, and average in fertility levels.

Planting

For most of the northern areas of the country, peppers need to be started indoors about eight to ten weeks before the last frost. They are slow to germinate and grow, so most people end up buying plants from the nursery. If you do start them yourself, make sure to harden them off by putting them outside for a longer time each day when the temperature is about fifty-five degrees. I usually wait until at least a week after the average last frost date to plant peppers in the garden. Just like tomatoes, you can plant them deeper than they were when growing in the pot.

Peppers will relish the warmest and sunniest spot in the garden. Since they are part of the nightshade family, do not plant them in soil that has grown tomatoes, eggplants, or potatoes in the last three years.

Plant them about eighteen to twenty-four inches apart, depending on variety; and it helps to stake the bell peppers as they can fall over or break branches when they get loaded with fruit.

Peppers are self-pollinating. So if you are saving seeds, make sure you separate your varieties (especially the hot peppers from the sweet ones). If you are not saving the seeds you do not have to worry about the cross pollination as it will not affect this years' fruit.

Watering

Consistent moisture is one of the keys to success with peppers. They like moist, but not wet soil.

Weeding

Because peppers are such a heat-loving plant, I always plant them through black landscape fabric. This also eliminates the need for weeding. If you plant them in the soil, keep them well weeded so as not to drain moisture away from the pepper plants.

Fertilizing

Peppers like phosphorus and calcium but not too much nitrogen. Excess nitrogen causes a nice, dark-green, bushy plant but not very many fruits. Once the plants start setting fruit, I will give them some compost tea every two weeks.

Harvesting

Peppers can be picked and eaten at any stage. I prefer the taste and texture of the mature red peppers, but I just can't resist early in the season so I do pick some green ones then. Also, I think the green jalapeños have a better taste than the red ones.

Storing

Peppers will store for about one to two weeks in the refrigerator, with green peppers storing longer than the red ones. I have had great luck freezing peppers and have stored them for a year with no problems. The good news is that freezing is easy to do since this is one of the few vegetables that does not require blanching first. Pick some nice, crisp peppers early in the morning and wash them. Cut them into strips, removing the stems, seeds, and any membrane. Put one layer of the strips on a tray in the freezer for an hour. Remove and store in a resealable bag in the freezer.

My family really likes pickled jalapeños, so that is how I store them. My secret there is to add a couple of cloves of garlic to the jar to give them a unique flavor.

Eating

Peppers are a staple in many of our meals, just like onions and garlic. We use them fresh in salads and dips and cooked in soups, stews, and salsas. One of my favorite meals is stuffed peppers made from fresh green (or preferably red) peppers filled with ground venison, tomato sauce, and brown rice.

POTATOES

I believe that potatoes are an important vegetable to grow in the home garden. First, the quality of a homegrown potato is vastly superior to anything found in a store. It is also very versatile in that it can be prepared in many different ways. A freshly harvested potato contains about 80 percent water and 20 percent dry matter. About 70 percent of the dry matter is starch and 10 percent is protein. It is a carbohydrate-rich food that contains vitamins B1, B3, B6, and C and the minerals potassium, phosphorus, and magnesium. Potatoes also contain antioxidants and are a good source of dietary fiber. Potatoes are now on the Dirty Dozen list in appendix B, as most of the commercially grown varieties are heavily laced with insecticides and fungicides.

Potatoes do their best in full sun, although I've had success in areas that are shaded in the morning.

Soil

Potatoes prefer a loose, well-drained sandy loam that has a high level of compost. This is one of the few vegetables that prefers a slightly acidic soil in the range of 5.8 to 6.5. I tend to put more time into building up the soil for potatoes than any other crop.

I start with a four-foot by eight-foot box, moving all of the soil from half of the box to the other half, down to a depth of eighteen to twenty-four inches. I will put in some wood ashes and organic fertilizer at the

FROM EARTH TO HEALTH

bottom and then add back the soil with some additional compost. I repeat that for the other side of the box.

Planting

The real key step that I've found to growing good potatoes is the proper selection of the seeds. Make sure to get certified seed potatoes, and don't use grocery store potatoes! They are almost always treated with a growth retardant. I prefer to use seeds (actually just small potatoes) that weigh around two ounces and have at least two growing eyes. If the seed potatoes do not have any eyes, place them in a single layer in a spot that is warm and has bright but indirect light. It will take several weeks for the eyes to begin to grow. If small, whole potatoes cannot be found, cut up the larger ones into pieces that have at least two eyes. I save my small potatoes from the year before to use for seed.

Although potatoes are a little frost-tolerant, I wait until a week or two before the last frost to plant. To plant the seed potatoes, I dig a trench about twelve inches deep in the center of a four-foot-wide box. Every eight inches, I dig a small hole about four inches deep and carefully plant a seed, covering it with compost. The eyes are very fragile at this point so be careful not to break them off. This is a little closer than most people plant them, but I'm not after big lunkers. I want a good quantity of medium-sized potatoes.

I have also had success planting potatoes in a round wire bin very similar to the ones I use to make compost. I will build a round wire bin about four feet in diameter and put in about twelve inches of good soil mixed with compost. Then I'll place eight or nine seeds in the center about eight inches apart and cover them with soil. When the vines get to be about a foot above the soil, I'll add about four inches more soil and continue to do that until the bin is almost full. Since the soil tends to dry out quickly in these bins, you will need to water more frequently.

Watering

Potatoes require a consistent amount of moisture during the growing season. Over-watered potatoes will have hollow or dark centers, and under-watered potatoes will be small or misshapen.

Weeding

Weeds are usually not a problem in the potato patch. By the time the weeds have germinated and started growing, it's time to either add some soil to the trench or bin; and the weeds just get covered up. And when the vines really get going, they should completely shade the soil.

Fertilizing

I do not add any fertilizer to potatoes during the growing season. The fertilizer that I placed below the seeds will supply all of the nutrients necessary for the plants.

Harvesting

Potatoes can be picked at any size, from the tiny new potatoes to the big lunkers. At the beginning of the season, I like to dig up one plant at a time. When those have been eaten, I go on to the next plant. For storage potatoes, pick between the time the tops die back and the first frost.

Newly picked potatoes are very fragile, so you must take care not to bruise or damage them when picking. I prefer to either do it by hand, if the soil is dry enough, or with a spading fork. Dig the fork into the soil to the side of the plant and gently pry the whole plant from the ground.

If any of the potatoes were growing above ground, they will turn green and you should not eat them as they are toxic. The toxin goes through the whole potato so it does no good to just trim off the green part.

Storing

There are many methods for storing potatoes. I like to store them in mesh bags (like an onion bag) in a cool, dark place that is fairly damp. A root cellar at forty to fifty degrees is perfect.

Eating

Our favorite way to eat potatoes is to slice them thinly and panfry them in olive oil and butter with some onions. It's also hard to beat a fresh, oven-baked potato, although mashed potatoes made with organic butter and raw goat milk come in a close second.

SPINACH

Spinach is a leafy green vegetable that grows best in cool weather. It is my second favorite vegetable, just behind kale. We usually associate spinach with iron and Popeye, but it is also packed with vitamins A ,C, E, and K as well as thiamine, potassium, and folic acid. Vitamin K is getting a lot of press lately for its use in coagulating blood and its ability to bind calcium to your bones. Spinach is one of the best sources of dietary vitamin K. There are eight different natural forms of vitamin E, and spinach is one of the few food sources that has all eight.

Spinach shares most of the growing traits of its cousin lettuce, but spinach is enough different to rate its own section. It is one of the easiest to grow of all vegetables, tolerating a wide range of soil, sun, and temperature conditions.

Soil

The best soil for spinach is light and has a high level of compost. Ideally the bed for spinach should be in full sun during the cooler months and partial sun during the heat of summer.

Planting

Spinach can be direct seeded into the garden as soon as the soil can be worked. For the first crop of the year, I start the plants indoors in soil blocks and transplant them into the garden when they are two to three weeks old. I continue to plant right through the summer, with the last planting in mid-September. This last planting is done in a hoophouse, and in a milder winter I can pick spinach right through the end of the year. During more severe winters, I let the crop go so that it will be the first harvest of the spring—usually right about the time I'm transplanting the new seedlings in April.

I generally don't give specific recommendations on plant varieties, but I've had phenomenal success with a spinach variety called Spargo. It has consistently outproduced and tasted better than any other variety of spinach I've ever planted.

Watering

Spinach is another shallow-rooted vegetable that needs consistent watering throughout the growing season.

Weeding

These vegetables grow so fast that they typically crowd out the weeds pretty well. I handpick any weeds I see so as not to combine them with the harvest.

Fertilizing

I have found that I get the best spinach by giving the plants a steady supply of nutrients, especially nitrogen. I alternate feeding every couple of weeks with my organic fertilizer and a foliar feed of fish emulsion.

Harvesting

I generally harvest spinach by picking individual leaves once they mature, or I cut the whole plant off about an inch above ground level. In either case the plants will continue to produce for many weeks.

Storing

Spinach can be stored unwashed in the refrigerator for two to three weeks. I find that it stores longer if you pick it first thing in the morning when the leaves still have dew on them. You can also freeze spinach by blanching it for no more than a minute, dunking it quickly into ice water, and letting it dry slightly before placing the leaves in freezer bags.

Eating

Spinach, unlike lettuce, can be eaten either fresh or cooked. We eat it fresh most of the time but also like it cooked in a Lebanese dish called *sleet*.

SQUASH

There are two categories of squash: winter and summer. Winter squash has thick skin and stores extremely well. Summer squash produces fruit with thin skins, does not store well, and the skins are typically not peeled when eaten. Butternut is a common type of winter squash, and zucchini is an example of summer squash.

Squash is a good source of vitamins B6 and E, thiamine, niacin, folate, calcium, and magnesium. It is a very good source of vitamins A and C, potassium, and manganese.

Squash is easy to grow, cold-tolerant, and very vigorous.

Soil

Squash, like all curcurbits, grows best in full sun and fertile soil. I have had good luck planting squash in a two-foot diameter by two-foot deep hole filled with finished compost.

Planting

Most types of squash are direct seeded. I push the envelope and start the plants three weeks before the last frost of the spring indoors in coconut coir pots under grow lights. At the same time, I'll put clear plastic over the garden spots where I will be planting the squash to warm up the soil.

Watering

Squash needs a lot of water, especially the winter varieties, as the vines can get quite long. (I've measured one at more than fifty feet long.) I even had one climb about twenty feet up an oak tree and got a lot of comments about my *squash tree*. If your squash leaves are drooping on a hot summer day, the plants are getting water-stressed. I give my plants a good soaking every other day during the summer.

Weeding

Happily I never weed the squash patch. I plant this vegetable through landscape fabric, and then I let the vines run outside the garden and down the hill. Some varieties of winter squash will send roots down from the stem, and this really helps to get nutrients and water to the whole plant.

Fertilizing

Squash plants are heavy feeders, so I'll give each plant about four to five gallons of compost tea every couple of weeks.

Harvesting

Summer squash needs to be harvested on a regular basis or the individual fruits get way too big. Frequent picking also stimulates more fruiting, although our problem is typically too much zucchini all at once.

Winter squash for storage needs to be completely ripe before you pick it. The fruit can withstand a light frost that can kill the vines, but a freeze that causes injury to the surface will rot the fruit in short order. Harvest the squash by cutting it with a sharp knife or lopping shears about two to three inches up the stem. A key item to long-term storage is to wash the fruit in soapy water containing one part chlorine bleach to ten parts of water. This removes the dirt and kills the surface pathogens that cause rotten spots.

Curing and Storage

Winter squash is cured at eighty to ninety degrees and 80 to 90 percent relative humidity for seven to ten days. I use a small bedroom and add an electric heater and humidifier. This curing hardens the skins, heals blemishes, and ripens fruit that may not be completely mature. The curing process is the same for sweet potatoes, so I do them at the same time.

After curing the squash, it should be stored in a cool, dark area at about fifty to fifty-five degrees and 50 to 70 percent humidity. If the humidity is too low, the flesh will dry out. If it is too high, it will cause a film of moisture that will quickly lead to rotting. Squash should not be stored on the floor or touching each other. Store squash away from apples, as the apples give off ethylene gas that decreases the shelf life of the squash. Inspect the squash regularly and remove any fruit that starts to rot because the pathogens will spread to the other fruit. Most varieties will store for three to four months using this system, but I have many squash that store for six months or more.

Eating

Summer squash is very versatile and you can use it in dips, salads, stir-fries, casseroles, and soups. Because of its delicate flavor, it can be added to almost any main dish. It is also used in many cake and bread recipes.

Winter squash is a staple for us, and we typically eat it baked or mashed. Although I don't grow pumpkins, we do use the winter squash in place of pumpkin in pies. Don't forget to roast the seeds as they are both tasty and a nutritional powerhouse.

Varieties

My two standard winter squash varieties that I grow every year are Waltham Butternut and Sunshine. Although Sunshine is an F1 hybrid, its taste, texture, and long storage life make it worth it. I have tried saving the seeds, resulting in some of the fruit looking a little weird but the flesh was still tasty.

SWEET POTATOES

Sweet potatoes are one of my primary crops (and no, they are not just for Thanksgiving dinner). These plants are part of the morning glory family and are not even related to the white potato. They are nutrient-dense, have high yields, and store extremely well if properly cured. According to the Center for Science in the Public Interest, the sweet potato is the number one most nutritious vegetable. The tender young shoots of the vine may also be eaten just like other greens.

Sweet potatoes are high in vitamins A and C and rich in calcium, folate, and potassium. The glycemic index is a low 17 (a white potato is 29 by comparison). One cup of sweet potatoes provides 26 percent of the recommended daily level of dietary fiber.

Many people think of them as a southern crop, but I have had great luck growing them in the north for many years. Most of the varieties require a growing season of one hundred days, but I do have a few tricks for growing them successfully here.

The biggest thing to know about sweet potatoes is that they are tropical plants and like it hot. They will not grow at all at a soil temperature of fifty degrees, and they require a minimum of sixty degrees to function. But they don't start thriving until seventy degrees and will do well all the way up to one hundred degrees.

The key to growing them in the north is to preheat the soil with clear plastic. I find the clear works better than the black; and if done properly, the weeds will not grow under the plastic. The trick is to thoroughly wet the soil first and then make sure the plastic is tight against the ground. (I bury the edges under the soil.)

Soil

Sweet potatoes prefer a light, sandy soil but will tolerate a fairly wide range of soil conditions. Too much fertility will result in some great-looking vines but not many sweet potatoes.

Planting

The part of the sweet potato that you plant is called a slip, which is a rooted cutting from a vine or, more commonly, a growth from the potato. You can grow the slips yourself by taking a sweet potato from last year's harvest (and they will last a year in storage), cutting off a one- or two-inch section from the top, and suspending it on toothpicks in a cup of water.

When the sprouts are a few inches long, break them off and put them in water. After a couple of weeks, roots will start to grow and you can now plant the slips in the ground. The best slips are about twelve inches long with five to six leaves and a strong stem. I typically wait until June 1 to plant my sweet potatoes because they just don't do well until both air and soil temperatures are nice and warm.

I have found that the best way to plant sweet potatoes is the exact opposite of regular potatoes: in a raised mound of soil instead of a trench. I cultivate a raised row about eight to twelve inches higher than the surrounding soil, with the rows being three feet apart. Then I create a shallow depression along the length of the row about one to two inches deep that makes it easy for the water to get to the plant roots.

Every twelve to fourteen inches, I'll cut a six-inch slit in the plastic and plant one of the slips, giving each one a good drink of warm water. I place each slip about four inches deep and make sure the terminal buds are aboveground.

Watering

Keep the soil moist for about the first month to develop a good root system. After that, water only during dry periods. The roots will rot if they are too wet.

Weeding

If you have planted through plastic, you'll never need to pick a weed. If you don't use plastic, the vines will soon cover the entire area and will shade out most weeds.

Fertilizing

Sweet potatoes don't require much fertility, so I do not add any fertilizer during the growing season.

Harvesting

Sweet potatoes don't mature; they just stop growing when the weather gets cold. Most of the varieties will be ready in about one hundred days after planting. The bulk of the growth takes place in the last two to three weeks, so you will want to let them grow as long as possible; but they do need to be harvested before the vines are killed by frost. I usually cover the vines with blankets at night starting in mid-September to get a few more weeks of growth.

On harvest day I remove all of the plastic and then carefully dig up the potatoes using a broadfork. If you nick any of the sweet potatoes, keep them separate and use them quickly as they will not store for long.

Curing and Storage

Unlike most vegetables, sweet potatoes are not very good when they are first picked (actually pretty dry and tasteless) because they need to be cured. After you dig the potatoes, get them out of the sun as soon as possible and cure them in an area that is eighty to ninety degrees with 80 to 90 percent relative humidity for seven to ten days. These are the same conditions as for winter squash, so I cure them together in a small room that I can put a heater and humidifier in. After curing store the tubers in a dark area with temperatures of fifty to sixty degrees. I separate out the smaller blemish-free potatoes to use for propagating the slips the next year.

Eating

We like our sweet potatoes baked (The skin is really good!) or fried in coconut oil. You may also mash them for use in casseroles and pies. I have found that they add a nice sweetness to venison stew.

Varieties

I've only tried a few varieties, but I've had the best success with the Beauregard variety.

TOMATOES

Tomatoes are the most popular garden crop in the United States. They are fairly easy to grow, don't require a large area, have high yields, and have many culinary uses.

Tomatoes are a very good source of vitamins A, C, and K as well as fiber, potassium, manganese, and magnesium. They are also rich in antioxidants, especially lycopene, which is the phytochemical that gives this fruit its red color.

Recent research has shown that cooking even enhances the lycopene content. Cooking usually degrades the vitamin and mineral content of fruits and vegetables, so this is good news for those of us who like tomato sauces and salsas.

Tomatoes come in two distinct types: determinate and indeterminate.

Determinate plants form compact bushes with shorter main stems. The fruits ripen all at the same time, and they tend to be more cold-tolerant. These plants need to be caged or staked, and you never want to pinch off any of the side shoots because this is where the fruits form.

Indeterminate plants will grow larger and higher until stopped or the frost gets them. They are best trained on strings or trellises so they can grow vertically. Pinch off the side shoots that emerge between the stalks and the leaf axils.

If you are growing tomatoes outdoors, you will need at least three to four months of warm weather and lots of sunshine.

Soil

The best soil for tomatoes is fertile and well-drained. A high level of organic matter and phosphorus will ensure a steady supply of moisture and nutrients.

A critical element of the soil overlooked by many tomato growers is the temperature. A tomato plant needs a root temperature of at least sixty degrees to grow properly. At fifty degrees the roots are not able to uptake the water and nutrients needed to survive. Between fifty and sixty degrees, the plants will just sit there and do nothing. Research has shown that the optimum soil temperature for tomatoes is seventy degrees.

Planting

I start my seedlings indoors under grow lights about six weeks before the last frost date. I start them in two-inch soil blocks and move them into four-inch blocks in about two weeks. By four weeks they are in a gallon root pouch. The root pouch is a reusable fabric pot that has all of the advantages of a soil block, but it won't fall apart. During the last two weeks, I put them out in the sun during the day and bring them back in at night. Not only does this harden off the plants, but exposing them to the wind makes their stalks much thicker and tougher. At this time I also put some black or clear plastic on the beds I will be planting the tomatoes in. This will preheat the soil and make it easier for the plants to get a good start.

If you cannot start your own seedlings and must buy them from a nursery, look for sturdy and compact plants that have a deep green color.

At transplant time I dig a one-foot diameter by one-foot deep hole and add some crushed eggshells in the bottom. (The calcium helps to prevent blossom end rot.) I plant the tomato right up to the level of the first true leaves, as the roots will grow out of the buried stem. I give most varieties a two-foot spacing between plants. If I have some tall, scraggly seedlings, I plant them horizontally because the top will naturally grow straight up. Then I backfill the hole with pure compost and give the plant a good drink of *warm* water.

Tomatoes like warm roots. Trim the bottom foot or so of leaves off when the plants get three to four feet high so that the sun can heat up the soil. This also helps prevent fungus problems by keeping the leaves clean.

Watering

Water the plants well the first couple of weeks after transplanting but then let the soil dry out some between waterings. When the fruits are ripening, there may be some tomatoes that split their skins if they get too much water all at once.

Weeding

I grow tomatoes through landscape fabric, so there is no weeding. If planted in soil, they grow so fast that weeds usually can't keep up after the first few weeks.

Fertilizing

Tomatoes are heavy feeders, and I like to given them a gallon of compost tea per plant once every other week. I make the tea by taking mature compost and letting it steep in water for several days. Then I strain it through cheesecloth. Occasionally I'll mix in some fish emulsion or liquid kelp.

Harvesting

Pick your tomatoes when they are fully ripe, and leave the stems on. Take care not to damage the skins as they can be fragile at this point. You can also pick tomatoes that are not quite ripe and put them in a dark, cool place to ripen.

Storing

The first rule of storing tomatoes is to never put them anywhere cold, as much of the flavor will be lost. A vine-ripened tomato should be stored at room temperature but only has a shelf life of four or five days after picking.

Once the tomato season really gets underway in August, we start processing them for long-term storage. Some get canned into sauce and juice; some are frozen; and some get cooked into chili, spaghetti sauce, and salsa.

Tomatoes may also be frozen whole, chopped, or pureed. Once frozen they must be cooked because they will be too mushy to eat as you would a fresh one.

Eating

Every year I just can't wait for the first ripe tomatoes of the summer. They are wonderful eaten right off the vine, and they are great in sandwiches and salads. One of my favorite lunches is a fresh tomato and swiss cheese sandwich.

Tomatoes can be cooked in a myriad of soups, stews, and salsas. We also make tomato and mixed-vegetable juices and can them.

*Varieties_*

I have trialed many varieties of tomatoes over the years, but the two I like the most are Amish Paste and Debarao. These are both paste-type tomatoes, but I like them in salads and sandwiches the best.

Appendix A

THE CLEAN FIFTEEN

According to the Environmental Working Group, these fifteen fruits and vegetables have the least amount of pesticides that have been tested for in 2012 (and updated annually at www.ewg.org):

- onions
- avocados
- sweet corn
- pineapples
- mangoes
- asparagus
- sweet peas
- kiwi
- cabbage
- eggplant
- papaya

- watermelons
- broccoli
- tomatoes
- sweet potatoes

Appendix B

THE DIRTY DOZEN

According to the Environmental Working Group, these twelve fruits and vegetables have the highest levels of pesticides that have been tested for in 2012:

- apples
- celery
- sweet bell peppers
- peaches
- strawberries
- nectarines
- grapes
- spinach
- lettuce
- cucumbers
- blueberries
- potatoes

Appendix C

RESOURCES

Ashworth, Suzanne. *Seed to Seed: Seed Saving and Growing Techniques for Vegetable Gardeners.* Seed Savers Exchange, 2002.

The best seed saving guide available.

Bubel, Mike and Nancy. *Root Cellaring: Natural Cold Storage of Fruits and Vegetables.* Storey Publishing, 1991.

Detailed manual for storing fruits and vegetables.

Campbell, Stu. *Let it Rot!* Vermont: Storey Publishing 1990.

A wonderful little book about composting for a garden.

Coleman, Eliot. *The Winter Harvest Handbook.* Chelsea Green Publications, 2009.

The bible when it comes to growing vegetables in unheated greenhouses.

Deppe, Carol. *The Resilient Gardener: Food Production and Self-Reliance in Uncertain Times.* Chelsea Green Publications, 2010.

A great study in how to grow great crops under all conditions.

Francis, Raymond. *Never Be Sick Again.* Health Communications, 2002.

Revolutionary but simple understanding of health and disease.

Jeavons, John. *How To Grow More Vegetables.* Ten Speed Press, 2006.

A comprehensive and detailed explanation of the biointensive method.

Pleasant, Barbara and Deborah Martin. *The Complete Compost Gardening Guide.* Storey Publishing, 2008.

A comprehensive guide to making and using compost.

Pollan, Michael. *The Botany of Desire.* Random House, 2001.

A plant's-eye view of the world.

Salatin, Joel. *Everything I Want to Do Is Illegal.* Polyface Inc., 2007.

How government regulations are stifling small farmers.

Solomon, Steve. *Gardening When It Counts: Growing Food in Hard Times.* New Society Publishers, 2006.

A good, basic organic gardening book.

Solomon, Steve. *The Intelligent Gardener {Growing Nutrient-Dense Food}*. New Society Publishers, 2013.

Everything you need to know about soil fertility.

Stell, Elizabeth. *Secrets to Great Soil*. Storey Publishing, 1998.

How to create healthy and fertile soil.

Made in the USA
Charleston, SC
23 April 2015